Showing Forth the Presence of God

Showing Forth the Presence of God

Joel S. Goldsmith

Edited by
Lorraine Sinkler

Acropolis Books, Publisher
Atlanta, Georgia

Published by Acropolis Books
All rights reserved
Printed in the United States of America

For information contact:
ACROPOLIS BOOKS, INC.
Atlanta, Georgia

www.acropolisbooks.com

Cover and text design: Tonya Beach Creative Services

Library of Congress Cataloging-in-Publication Data

Goldsmith, Joel S., 1892-1964.
  Showing forth the presence of God / Joel S. Goldsmith ; edited by
Lorraine Sinkler.
    p. cm.
  Includes bibliographical references.
  ISBN 1-889051-69-1 (alk. paper)
  1. Presence of God--Miscellanea. 2. New Thought. I. Sinkler,
Lorraine. II. Title.

BP610.G64174 2005
299'.93--dc22
                                        2004026972

Except the Lord build the house,
they labour in vain that build it. . .

— Psalm 127

"Illumination dissolves all material ties and binds men together with the golden chains of spiritual understanding; it acknowledges only the leadership of the Christ; it has no ritual or rule but the divine, impersonal universal Love; no other worship than the inner Flame that is ever lit at the shrine of Spirit. This union is the free state of spiritual brotherhood. The only restraint is the discipline of Soul; therefore, we know liberty without license; we are a united universe without physical limits, a divine service to God without ceremony or creed. The illumined walk without fear – by Grace."

—*The Infinite Way* by Joel S. Goldsmith

Dedication

Twentieth century mystic Joel S. Goldsmith revealed to the Western world the nature and substance of mystical living that demonstrated how mankind can live in the consciousness of God. The clarity and insight of his teachings, called the Infinite Way, were captured in more than thirty-five books and in over twelve hundred hours of tape recordings that, today, perpetuate his message.

Joel faithfully arranged to have prepared from his class tapes, monthly letters which were made available as one of the most important tools to assist students in their study and application of the Infinite Way teachings. He felt each of these letters came from an ever-new insight that would produce a deeper level of understanding and awareness of truth as students worked diligently with this fresh and timely material.

Each yearly compilation of the *Letters* focused on a central theme, and it became apparent that working with an entire year's material built an ascending level of consciousness. The *Letters* were subsequently published as books, each containing all the year's letters. The publications became immensely popular as they proved to be of great assistance in the individual student's development of spiritual awareness.

Starting in 1954, the monthly letters were made availiable to students wishing to subscribe to them. Each year of the *Letters* was published individually during 1954 through 1959 and made available in book form. From 1960 through 1970 the *Letters* were published and renamed as books with the titles:

1960 Letters	*Our Spiritual Resources*
1961 Letters	*The Contemplative Life*
1962 Letters	*Man Was Not Born to Cry*
1963 Letters	*Living Now*
1964 Letters	*Realization of Oneness*
1965 Letters	*Beyond Words and Thoughts*
1966 Letters	*The Mystical I*
1967 Letters	*Living Between Two Worlds*
1968 Letters	*The Altitude of Prayer*
1969 Letters	*Consciousness Is What I Am*
1970 Letters	*Awakening Mystical Consciousness*

Joel worked closely with his editor, Lorraine Sinkler, to ensure each letter carried the continuity, integrity, and pure consciousness of the message. After Joel's transition in 1964, Emma A. Goldsmith (Joel's wife) requested that Lorraine continue working with the monthly letters, drawing as in the past from the inexhaustible tape recordings of his class work with students. The invaluable work by Lorraine and Emma has ensured that this message will be preserved and available in written form for future generations. Acropolis Books is honored and privileged to offer in book form the next eleven years of Joel's teaching.

The 1971 through 1981 *Letters* also carry a central theme for each year, and have been renamed with the following titles:

1971 Letters	*Living by the Word*
1972 Letters	*Living the Illumined Life*
1973 Letters	*Seek Ye First*
1974 Letters	*Spiritual Discernment: the Healing Consciousness*
1975 Letters	*A Message for the Ages*
1976 Letters	*I Stand on Holy Ground*
1977 Letters	*The Art of Spiritual Living*
1978 Letters	*God Formed Us for His Glory*
1979 Letters	*The Journey Back to the Father's House*
1980 Letters	*Showing Forth the Presence of God*
1981 Letters	*The Only Freedom*

Acropolis Books dedicates this series of eleven books to Lorraine Sinkler and Emma A. Goldsmith for their ongoing commitment to ensure that these teachings will never be lost to the world.

Table of Contents

Showing Forth the Presence of God

Chapter One

Lift Yourself to a
Spiritual Altitude

Everybody is seeking a way out of human limitation, human failure, and human conditions, all the difficulties of human life. We, that is, those who have any degree of social awareness or social sensitivity are not only seeking a way out of lack and limitation for ourselves; we are seeking a way out of lack and limitation for all the nations that do not have abundance. We are not only seeking a way out of ill health for ourselves, we are seeking to find health and harmony for all the peoples of the world. We are not only seeking to find peace in our individual lives, we are also seeking to find peace for all peoples on the face of the earth. When I say, "we," I am speaking of all of us, in this work or out, in orthodox religions or unorthodox religions, and of those who have no religion.

Every thinking person is seeking a way out of human difficulties and out of human limitation, not only for themselves, but for all the world. This concern has been going on for many, many centuries, and the wonder is that in all these centuries a way has not been found to take us out of these difficulties, these problems, and these human miseries. When we look around to investigate what means are being used to overcome world difficulties, we find that these means are usually on a material level.

We have been trying to meet the needs of the world by means of all the material resources of the universe, by means of invention, science, and discovery. It is a turning to whatever exists in the material realm.

Attempts to Solve Problems
by Supernatural Means

There are a few who turn to some particular concept of God and fare no better than those who resort only to material means. We may wonder at that until through research we discover that when the world was sparsely populated with only a few native tribes here and there on different continents and islands, and living without any religion, as the problems of human living became acute and unsolvable, some of the thinking members of these tribes began to look for another solution, a solution that might possibly be found outside of human means.

Eventually, they discovered something they thought of as a deity or a God. The question then arose: How could they bring that God into their experience? If there were a drought, how could they get God to give them rain? If their neighbor insisted on warring with them, how could they get God to make them victorious over their enemies? If there were no fish in the sea, how could they get God to increase the supply of fish, or the number of cattle on a thousand hills?

Out of such questions came many of the methods now in use. Then came the idea of tithing with God, giving God ten percent to see if He would not give ninety percent in return for the ten. Evidently, when asking God or tithing with God did not produce all the answers, another way had to be found.

So they turned to sacrifices. Sacrifice became a way of trying to wheedle out of God what God was not giving them: the sacrifice of money to the temples, the sacrifice of doves, the sacrifice of lambs, the sacrifice of crops, and eventually human sacrifice. First, they sacrificed babies, but theirs was a strange God, and babies were not enough, so adults were sacrificed. Along with these sacrifices were rites, rituals, and ceremonies, designed to make God open up this infinite storehouse of supply, protection, and good.

Gradually, all these practices were incorporated into the religions of the world, so that we have had asceticism, sacrifices, and prayers in many different forms, tithing or bribing God, or building temples to please and placate Him. In modern times, to all intents and purposes the only practice that has been given up is human sacrifice and the sacrifice of live animals. Otherwise, all the rituals, rites, prayers, ceremonies, asceticism, and sacrifices have been incorporated into most modern religious teachings. Still the problems of the world have not lessened. Rather have they multiplied.

Is There a Spiritual Solution?

In this modern age, as in the past, we are seeking the solution to the world's problems in material force or other material forms—money, agreements, properties—and finding no answer. No wonder, then, that throughout this world the thinkers of today are trying to find another solution to the problems of the world, and in some cases, solutions that at least are helpful have been found insofar as individual experience is concerned and also in the experience of small groups and communities. Up to this moment, the solution to the world's problems has not been demonstrated on a world-wide scale in any area. Therefore, we can speak only of what has been demonstrated on a scale measurable by those who have turned themselves to another solution of their human problems individually and collectively.

Today, the idea of a spiritual solution to individual and collective problems is very seriously being considered, not only in the unorthodox religious movements, but certainly in orthodox religions as well, and eventually, of course, it is there that success will be achieved. As was promised early in this century, the secret of spiritual power and how to bring it into our affairs individually and collectively has been discovered.

Old Concepts of God Must Be Given Up for a God of Spirit

First of all, our concepts of God must be changed. We have to give up the idea of a God that is going to interfere in our affairs because we go through certain ceremonies or rites of worship, or the idea of a God who is going to respond to us because we have become ascetic in our living. It has been proved that that kind of an approach does not work, that such a concept of God is not God. Therefore, the very first undertaking of a thinker, seeking to solve either individual or collective problems, is to take the attitude: since there is something within me that tells me beyond all doubt that there is a God, that God is, and since I have no doubt about God's existence, the riddle for me is to discover that God and how to approach It.

One thing is certain. God is invisible: God has never been reached through the human mind; no one has ever been able intellectually to know what God is, or even to know how God functions. No one in all these thousands of years has ever been able to pray to God with the mind and receive very much of a response. God is Spirit, and it naturally follows that prayer must be spiritual. But if prayer is spiritual, it cannot be of the mind. If God is Spirit, the approach to God must be spiritual, and if we do not know what Spirit is, we will not know what a spiritual approach is.

If we try to think this thing through, eventually we come to a dead end, and for the same reason. No one has ever reached God through the mind, and it seems quite likely that no one ever will. God must be reached through the Spirit, by spiritual means, and this bars the use of words and thoughts as a means

of understanding God. This, for most of us, makes prayer difficult, if not impossible.

The Mind of Man Cannot Know God

Even though I can give you the revelation that has been
given to me, it can serve you only in the degree that it brings
forth a response within you, so that you, yourself, may be able
to experience God through prayer. No words written on these
pages will give you the secret. The secret is not to be given
through words or through thoughts. If you receive the secret as
you read this letter, you will receive it, not through the words
that are written, but through the Spirit that flows forth with the
words and the thoughts. In other words, there must be within
you a spiritual discernment, just as there must flow out from me
a spiritual consciousness, because God is Spirit, and there is no
way to impart God or the wisdom of God through words or
thoughts, but only through the Spirit.

An example of the necessity of spiritual discernment came
when the Master asked his disciples, "Whom do men say that I
the Son of man am? And they said, Some say that thou art John
the Baptist; some, Elias; and others, Jeremiah, or one of the
prophets,"[1] indicating clearly that the idea of reincarnation was
accepted in the Christian world as well as in the Oriental world.
The disciples, in their response to Jesus, recognized that men
were basing their evaluation of Jesus on their intellectual
insight.

A second time, the Master turned to the disciples, and this
time he did not say, "Whom do men say that I am?" but,
"Whom say ye that I am?"[2] "Men" and "ye" are quite different,
because in that question Jesus as much as said, "*Ye* are my disciples; *ye* have been with me some time; *ye* have seen that I speak
a different language." And so Peter could answer, "Thou art the
Christ, the Son of the living God. And Jesus answered and said
unto him, . . . Flesh and blood hath not revealed it unto thee."[3]

By that he meant his identity could not be known by men through the mind, the intellect, or through books. It was as if he were telling them in so many words, "The Father within, that is, spiritual awareness, spiritual discernment, and spiritual capacities discern, that while outwardly I may be a Hebrew rabbi, inwardly I am spiritually ordained, the Son of God, or the Christ. But this you cannot tell by looking at me or my gown, and that is why men are fooled. They hear my words or they see this robe, but you who have this inner capacity for discernment, you have rightly discerned."

Only Spiritual Endowment Reveals God

Before we can avail ourselves of God's blessings, God's grace, God's presence, and God's power we must know God. To know Him aright is life eternal—not to have some concept of God, not some belief or faith in God. Nothing can be gained from a concept, a belief, or a faith. It is knowing God aright that is life eternal. We do not know God aright from anything that we are told or anything that we read. These only put us on the track of discovery, the track leading to the experience. We know God only when the experience of God takes place within us, so that like the blind man who was healed we can say, "One thing I know, that, whereas I was blind, now I see."[4]

The words that I write or speak will not impart the nature of God or prayer, but the Spirit, the Consciousness, the awareness given me will utter Itself, and then if, like Peter, a person has the spirit of discernment, a receptivity, it will register within him, and he will be able to realize, "This is truth; this is it," and he will experience it. Only the experience brings the fruitage. No man can give God to another, but those, who are in any degree spiritually endowed or have in any degree received some measure of knowing God aright, can impart this through the Spirit to those of discernment. God is Spirit, and our contact with God must be a spiritual one, not a contact of the mind, not of words, not of thoughts. This again brings up the question, How?

How Do We Love God?

My experience is that God is reached only through the intent of the heart, in other words, the motive. We are told, "And thou shalt love the Lord thy God with all thine heart, and with all thy soul, and with all thy might."[5] Why heart? What is the meaning of "with all thine heart"? It has nothing to do with a fleshly organ, that we all know. Then what does it mean, "with all thine heart"?

Let us bring that language down to our own experience and let us assume that I am saying to you, "I love you with all my heart." What do you imagine I mean by that, "I love you with all my heart"? I can have only one meaning. I mean that I love you purely; I love you without motive; I love you without an idea of gain; I love you without any purpose in mind except I just love you. That is all. No reason, no hope for a return, no desire for anything on my part. I just love you. Because of that purity of motive, if that purity is there, I would say, "I love you with all my heart." To love God with all our heart can only mean to love God so purely that our love has in it no taint of desire for a return, no taint of self-interest, no taint of selfishness.

How can I love God that way? How is it possible? It either has to be possible or it is outside the realm of reality, of truth. How can I love God that way? I can love God in that way only if I can rise above my personal sense of selfhood, that is, my selfish sense.

Spiritual Ignorance

In our spiritual ignorance and ignorant forms of worship, we pray to God for something for you, for Mrs. Jones, Mr.

Smith, or for me. In our spiritual ignorance, we actually believe that there is a God that will answer such prayers. In our spiritual ignorance, we pray to God, "Prosper my country. Help me defeat my enemy." Of course, my enemy may be in the right and may have justice on his side but, "God, pay no attention to that. Let my side be victorious," the Red, White, and Blue, the Stars and Stripes forever, or whatever the particular flag or religion may be. This is the prayer of spiritual ignorance, because there can be no such God.

Once we enter the realm of a spiritual thinker, we must know that if there is a God at all, there can be only one God, and if there is only one God, it would have to be your God and my God. That would have to be true whether we are Jew or Gentile, Catholic or Protestant, Oriental or Occidental. It would also have to be true if we were saint or sinner, probably a little bit more true if we are a sinner, because we would need God more. But above all things, the person who has begun even to reach the hem of spiritual realization would know that there is only one God, so there would be no use in praying to God for the benefit of one person as against another, or the benefit of one race or nation against another.

Every election day, when I see pictures in the paper of the candidates going to church to pray before the election, I think of what a quandary God must be in. Probably not one of the candidates is worthy of being elected, nevertheless, all of them are confident that there is a God that will see them through.

Praying Spiritually

To pray spiritually, to pray with all our heart and all our soul, to pray purely, then, means that our prayer must be wholly universal. It must be that God's grace reach the consciousness of every individual. If a person is a sinner, it must reach that consciousness to free him from sin or desire. If it is fear that is holding him, then God must reach that consciousness to release him from fear. If it is domination or tyranny, God must reach that consciousness. In other words, there can be no prayer that has any other motive than that the kingdom of God be established on earth as it is in heaven. Any other prayer is a materialistic concept of prayer with a materialistic concept of God, or the old concept of God as some kind of a superhuman being that has a favorite race, religion, or nation.

"To love the Lord thy God with all thine heart" means actually to pray purely, from a pure motive, the pure desire that God's grace touch the consciousness of mankind. It must be the pure realization that God is in the midst of me, not meaning "me," Joel, but all the me's and you's that exist around this world, including the you of the past, the present, and the future, because everyone who has ever lived lives now. Everyone who ever will live lives now. If he is born a hundred generations from now, it is only because he is living now. The prayer, therefore, that does not include those of what in time and space we call the past, the present, and the future is not a prayer, because it is addressed to a finite concept of God, instead of the realization that God is in the midst of every "me." But who is this "me"? If God in the midst of me is not in the midst of every "me" in the past, present, and future, then God is nowhere present.

But if there is one thing that intellectually can be said of God truthfully, it is that God is omnipresence. If we cannot approach the one true God in human terms, at least we can understand omnipresence, and omnipresence must mean Allpresence: past presence, present presence, and future presence, omnipresence within every person now and always. "The place whereon thou standest is holy ground."[6] If that remark were addressed to one special person, one race of people, one nation of people, or one religion, it would be sacrilege in the face of God. But, if it is true that "the place whereon thou standest is holy ground," it is only because God is omnipresent.

Scripture says, "If I ascend up into heaven, thou art there: if I make my bed in hell, behold, thou art there. If I take the wings of the morning, and dwell in the uttermost parts of the sea; Even there shall Thy hand lead me, and thy right hand shall hold me."[7] The I it is talking about must be all the enemy I's as well as all the friendly I's. In addition to "Love the Lord thy God with all thine heart" must also follow the dictum to love our neighbor with all our heart. Therefore, if we are to love our neighbor as ourself, we could not declare omnipresence for ourself without declaring omnipresence everywhere present.

Prayer as an Open, Receptive Consciousness

It is possible to bring spiritual power into our experience. There are some millions of people on earth who have proved and are proving that spiritual power is effective in matters of health, supply, peace, and human relationships. But those people have a far different idea of God than the concept of God that can do something for me or mine and leave out you and yours. First of all, must come the inner feeling that where I am, God is. But if we believe that that is true only of this finite space, we are trying to finitize God. Unless we see this universally, we do not understand God, and we are certainly not loving God purely, nor are we loving our neighbor as our self.

If even a grain of what I am saying is perceived, the next step is simple. This universe which we see cannot be the universe of God's creating because, since God is Spirit, God's creation must be spiritual. If God is invisible, God's creation is invisible. We see only a finite concept of God's creation, but at least from observing certain aspects of nature, we must realize the omnipresence of God, the all-wisdom, the all-knowingness of God, and this prepares us for prayer.

To begin with, if we have selfishness in our heart, that is, a desire to satisfy the self, it is not going to be prayer and it is not going to reach God. Secondly, if it includes any desire to tell or enlighten God, it also has no element of prayer in it, for if God is not omniscience, then God does not know enough to fulfill our needs. Let us for a moment accept, even if we cannot quite grasp it, the fact that a God that could create anything appearing in as many miraculous ways as this world, with all its laws of nature, science, mathematics, and divine principles, any God capable of that must be capable of knowing our need before we do. Therefore, to approach God with any idea of achieving conscious God-contact must be to approach God in that understanding.

> God is omniscience; therefore, Father, forgive this
> erring mind if it tries to enlighten You, to tell You, or
> to ask You for anything.

A prayer is an open, receptive state of consciousness, acknowledging that whatever wisdom there is must come from God to man, not go from man to God. Are such prayers answered? I come back to you with the original statement: depending on the purity of the motive. God does not hear our words or read our thoughts, but God does know the intents of our heart, the motive in our heart, and God is omniscience. Let no one believe he is fooling God. Fool man? Yes, and even then, not all the men all of the time, according to Lincoln.

We cannot fool all men always. We cannot fool God at any time, in any way, because God is not a superman; God is the consciousness of this universe; God is the substance of which this universe is formed. When we approach God it is as if—and I am using a material symbol, I do not mean it literally—it is as if God were the film of a camera, and He is photographing our heart, and be assured that what is in that heart is going to show up. There is no way to have one thing in the heart and have another picture reach the mind of God.

Go to God With a Pure Heart

There is an answer to prayer—there really is. But it is when we can go to God knowing that the intent of my heart is that

God's grace be experienced by me, by you, by the friends, by the enemies, by the saints, but above all, by the sinners. The Master made it clear that to love them which love you is selfishness, personal interest, self-interest. We must pray for our enemies if we would be children of God. Why would we like to be children of God? Because if we are children of God, we are heirs of God. How good it is to be an heir. How beautiful it is to gain our good by inheritance instead of by the sweat of our brow. How nice it is to receive our good by a divine grace. If we would be an heir of God, a child of God, one way of accomplishing it is to pray for our enemies.

That is what I mean when I exhort students to go to God with a pure heart, not that my fellow religionists be benefited, not that my family or my nation be benefited, but that God's grace may bring freedom. Those who pray aright, those who find contact with the Spirit do find their freedom from fear, from sin, disease, and from lack. The Bible is not really fictional when it says, "He that dwelleth in the secret place of the most High shall abide under the shadow of the Almighty. . . . There shall no evil befall thee, neither shall any plague come nigh thy dwelling."[8] The Master was not misleading his followers when he said, "He that abideth in me, and I in him, the same bringeth forth much fruit. . . . If a man abide not in me, he is cast forth as a branch, and is withered."[9] In order for us to receive the grace of God, we must be one with God. We cannot be one with God if we are seeking something only for ourselves, for "God is no respecter of persons."[10]

We have misled ourselves through following centuries of teachings that attempt to maintain us on a material level and at the same time turn us to a spiritual God, such as thinking of God as Spirit, but that we also need money or health. The two, God as Spirit and the physical universe, do not team up. To enter prayer spiritually, it is necessary to identify ourselves with a spiritual atmosphere.

Lift Yourself Above the Mortal Concept of Self to the Kingdom Within

Let us consider for a moment the word, "I." In the human picture, if I say, "I," I am referring to Joel, and if you say, "I," you are referring to whatever your name is. But that is mistaken identity. *I* is not Joel, and *I* is not Bill, Mary, Jones, or Smith. *I* is a spiritual entity, spiritual being, spiritual Selfhood, and if we would enter the realm of spiritual prayer, the kingdom of God, we must take no thought for our life, but seek the kingdom of God, and then the things will be added. We are to seek the spiritual realm, the spiritual atmosphere, the spiritual kingdom, and when we open our eyes, the things we thought we needed are all provided. How are we to seek the kingdom of God? The only way we can do it is to start where we are, and that is with the word, "I."

"I and my Father are one,"[11] and that Father is Spirit.
Therefore, I am spiritual.
What am I doing then, groveling around
and begging for a little food, clothing, or housing?
God is Spirit; I am one with Spirit; I am spiritual.
I am of the household of God;
I am of the family of God, heir of God,
child of God.

"Son, thou art ever with me, and all that I have is
thine."[12] The spiritual kingdom is mine, and I am
groveling in the dirt to try to get rid of a headache,
a toe ache, to get a place to sleep,
or a few dollars more. God is Spirit.
"Son, thou art ever with me." Then I am in God's
kingdom. I am in the spiritual realm; I am in
spiritual consciousness; I am one with the Father.
Where God is, I am; where the Father is, I am.

We must lift ourselves up out of the material concept of existence. Just as we must rise above the traditional material concept of God and prayer, so we must overcome the material concept of ourselves and identify ourselves with God.

By lifting ourselves into the spiritual realm, we find ourselves in a whole new consciousness, no longer in a consciousness of lack and limitation at any level, no longer in a consciousness of being cut off from the world with four billion people against us or competing with us, no longer in a hostile atmosphere. This is the new consciousness in which we have lifted ourselves up above the mortal concept of self into the kingdom of God. There is only one way to get there: through our consciousness.

> I consciously dwell with God; I live and have my being in God, with God. I dwell "in the secret place of the most High." I abide in the Word, and the Word abides in me. God is my dwelling place; God is my high tower; God is my fortress. I live, and move, and have my being in Him. I am spiritual, the offspring of the most High. I am the son of God.

Truth Is Always Universally Applicable

We must always remember that whatever of truth we are realizing for ourselves is also the truth about our friends and neighbors, our friendly neighbors and our enemy neighbors, our saintly neighbors and our sinful neighbors. Whether or not we have been hypnotized by world sense into believing that we are groveling beggars, worms in the dust, or the prodigal, the truth is that we are one with the Father and heir of the Father. Can we be more of a prodigal than the Prodigal Son, who, when he turned around, found the Father walking out to meet him? Are we more of a prodigal than the woman taken in adultery, more than the thief on the cross? All of these found their way back to the Father-consciousness.

In our human sense, we are all prodigals, and even the most righteous on earth are prodigals. As long as we think we are good, as long as we think we are righteous, as long as we think we are religious, we are prodigals. Until we can truthfully say, "Why callest thou me good?"[13] and mean it in our heart and not hold back a little reservation, "Oh, well, after all, I am pretty good, pretty benevolent, or pretty kind," we are that prodigal-state of consciousness.

Spiritual wisdom is to be able to realize that any good that has ever flowed through us must be God's will and God's grace. We have been only the instrument for it. As Paul said, "For the good that I would I do not: but the evil which I would not, that I do. Now if I do that I would not it is no more I that do it, but sin that dwelleth in me."[14] In other words, whatever of an erroneous nature we have done has not been our nature. In our ignorance we have been victimized, and we have let ourselves be instruments for evil. But we are not evil, because the only *I* there is has always dwelt with God. The *I* that goes up to heaven is the *I* that never left heaven, and that is the *I* that we are.

The journey from the Father's house to the feast with the swine is not a real journey at all. It is not anybody going any place or returning. It is a dream. It has been called the Adam-dream, the dream-experience. And which is the greater dream: the sleeping dream or the waking dream? They are both of the same nature, as we learn when we awaken in His likeness. When we awaken to the truth, "I and my Father are one. . . . Son, thou art ever with me, and all that I have is thine," then we realize that we never journeyed any place: we slept, we dreamed.

The Journey to Illumination Is Encompassed in a Moment of Awakening

Those who are dead in sleep are the unillumined. The unillumined are not going anywhere, and when they become illumined, they still have not gone anywhere. They have just awakened. This is not a journey in time or space; this is not a journey from one place to another. This is a journey within the Soul; and in reality it is not even a journey. That is not even the right word. It is just a sleeping or an awakening. It is either spiritual ignorance or spiritual illumination, but it takes place here where we are when it does take place. That is why the Master could reveal that the kingdom of God is not in a holy mountain or a holy temple. The kingdom of God is not "Lo here! Or, Lo there! For, behold, the kingdom of God is within you.[15]. . . Awake thou that sleepest, and arise from the dead."[16]

Before his awakening, Paul was Saul of Tarsus, the unillumined: he is St. Paul when he is illumined, the same man: asleep, asleep and unillumined, but then awake and illumined. The Master was a Hebrew rabbi, and then he became the Christian savior; Gautama the Buddha, a temporal prince, a beggar, a seeker, and an ascetic, unillumined, and the next moment he is not Gautama: he is the Buddha, the enlightened one, the same man at one time unenlightened and then enlightened. Is it not the history of all our mystics, unenlightened one moment, the same man enlightened the next moment?

All the journeys Gautama took were taken only because they were necessary for his particular unfoldment. Actually, it should have been possible to awaken even while a prince in his father's court, but because that set up a sense of limitation in him, he had to wander out to find it.

This is the story of the Holy Grail and also of the Bluebird. After we have spent our fortune, worn out our clothing and everything else, and returned home, broken in purse and in health, we find the Bluebird singing up in our tree or the Holy Grail hanging in our back lot. It is the story of everyone who has received any measure of spiritual light. They found it within their own consciousness, because that is where the word of God is. Awaken and hear it! But it can only be done when we love the Lord our God with all our heart and our neighbor as ourself, when our love is pure, when it is not a question of "I am coming to you, God, to heal my body, to increase my supply, or for some other purpose." It has not worked in all these thousands of years, so why should we keep on with it? Let us give up seeking God for a purpose and let our search be for the kingdom of God.

Instruments for God's Expression

"And this is life eternal, that they might know thee the only true God."[17] Therefore, our whole aim should be to know God, not afar off, but within us. If we turn to teachers, teachings, or books, it is only that they may be the bridge that we walk over to return to the spirit of God that is within us, not that we should deify a teacher, a teaching, or a book, but that we should think of these as bridges leading us back to the kingdom of God within. We honor and respect the teacher, the teaching, and the book, but we worship only the God that dwells within us, until eventually we come, as St. Paul did, to the great realization, "Why, this is not my life at all. I could have found God on the first day of my search, had somebody only told me that this is not my life at all, but that God is living my life." In that awareness we relax and let it happen. We relax and receive God's wisdom, God's grace, God's peace. We can never really have any peace, wisdom, or grace of our own, and so it is better to surrender in the first place than in the last.

"I live; yet not I, but Christ liveth in me."[18] When we understand God as the divine, universal Consciousness, the substance and the law of all creation, then we can understand how it is that God formed us, mind and body, as instruments for His expression that He may express Himself as individual life.

Chapter Two

Freedom By Grace

Man shall not live by bread alone, but by every word
that proceedeth out of the mouth of God.

Matthew 4:4

In our human experience, we live primarily by our own efforts,
by virtue of air, food, water, and investments. We live by all
the things of the outer world.

Almost from the beginning of time, it has been known that
while this materialistic way of life may result in the attaining of the
things we seek, it seldom brings real satisfaction after they have
been attained. Although living in the world with a total reliance on
the things of the outer world does sometimes result in the attainment of what we may have been seeking, it usually leaves us frus-
trated because we have neither become complete in ourselves, nor
have we attained an inner satisfaction or a sense of rightness.

Material Progress Does Not
Necessarily Conflict With Spiritual Values

For this very reason, throughout all time there have been
those few persons devoted to something higher than material

accomplishments. Referring to the material good of this world, however, as "just material accomplishments" is not meant to place it in the category of the unnecessary or the evil. Let us not make the mistake of believing that there is no value in these great accomplishments on the material level, because that is nonsensical. The world is better off than in any previous generation, because of the invention, science, discovery, exploration, mining, and research that have been going on for years. We need not decry these material advances. The tragedy is that our moral and spiritual development has not kept pace with our material achievements.

I realize that too often we hear discussions and read articles or books giving the impression that materialism is some kind of an evil, that the development, as well as the conservation, of our natural resources, and the discoveries of the many conveniences which we enjoy today in some way are wrong. To take such an attitude is to revert in a measure, at least, to the idea of ascetism. There is no virtue whatsoever in ascetism, nor did the Master himself preach or practice leaving this world.

Certainly the scientific advances in all areas of our life are products of underlying spiritual principles or they could not have been brought forth into manifestation. The automobile, the airplane, business machines—all these exist only because there are principles on which they operate. Some of these, of course, have been used by man for wrong purposes, but that does not make the discovery and right use of them wrong.

A Well-Rounded Life

One purpose of the religious life should be to bring out greater and greater discoveries, greater and greater inventions for the benefit of mankind, while at the same time developing the moral and spiritual capacities of an individual so that the contributions of inventive genius will be rightly used and for the universal benefit rather than for the benefit of a few.

A well-rounded life, which is the life that all of us are really seeking and striving to attain, must be one of outer accomplishment as well as inner attainment. When the outer accomplishments are the result of our inner attainments and when the purity of our inner desires guides us to bring forth invention, discovery, and research for the welfare of mankind, then we not only individually lead a well-rounded life, but we help make for the people of this world a well-rounded life.

Mass Thinking Stultifies Individual Creativity

It is sad, nevertheless true, and it must be faced, that when people merge their identity in the mass-consciousness, they, in and of themselves, have no capacity for thinking, no capacity even for desiring to go in a right direction. A great responsibility rests upon those who have released from within the natural gift of intelligence and ability to invent, to develop art, and to carry on scientific experiments. These gifts must be accompanied by the necessary moral and spiritual qualities that will enable them to lead those who have not learned how to release that innate capacity and who, therefore, are not yet capable of creating these benefits for themselves.

The masses are unthinking, not that they do not have the capacity to think, but because they have never had the education and training that would enable them to develop these hidden capacities. These can never be rightly developed until a spiritual awakening takes place in them. Those who have attained spiritual awareness also possess other capacities: capacities for art, literature, science, discovery, research, invention. Of course, it would be a great blessing for the world if all thinkers had spiritual capacity, but it is fortunate that many of those who have spiritual capacity also have these other qualities. This at least leads us in the direction in which we are going now, that place where eventually everyone will understand his own nature and make use of his capacities.

The Role of Education

What is it that makes some persons susceptible to the destructive ideas of certain ideologies? What is it that makes so many persons susceptible to limiting ideas? The belief is entertained by many persons that people are educated because we have a free press and free schools with education available to all. This is the error. It does not. It may give them facts, some of which they have not developed the capability of absorbing, but it does not educate them. It does not lead them out of their narrow, limited views to the wider horizons awaiting the truly educated.

No one can be truly educated until his faculties are awakened, the faculties that enable him, not only to accept, but to assimilate and evaluate knowledge and information. A parrot can say two times two is four, but it cannot do anything with it. The mass of mankind is like that. It can repeat statements, but it does not understand them: it cannot digest them; it cannot assimilate them, because the faculties that would enable a person to drink in wisdom are not yet awakened.

The responsibility lies with religious leaders, as well as school teachers, to awaken those faculties so that when knowledge and information are placed before these individuals they can accept and understand it.

Teaching Individual Worth

How are these faculties best developed? Experience reveals that the moment an individual, even as a child, begins to perceive the nature, character, dignity, and individuality of his own being, these inner faculties begin to awaken. The first step in education must be to awaken individuals, whether children or adults, to the fact that individually they are important, that individually they are God-created, that individually they count, that everyone that exists in this world exists at the standpoint of divine Sonship. Each one is a soul, an individual with the rights to life, liberty, and the pursuit of happiness. This is the foundation on which a people can receive education and know what to do with it.

The tendency in the last two generations has been the opposite of this, to try to convince people that they are nothing. Trade unions have played a part in the curtailment of individual freedom. But trade unions, in and of themselves, should not be considered an evil. There is a rightful purpose and place for them, but they have become evil because, in many cases, no one had a voice in the decisions made except the men at the top, requiring everyone to be subservient to the top leadership. This was the beginning which later made it possible to feed these people ideas which were destructive to individual liberty and freedom, making them an easy prey to being nothing. They became susceptible to mass propaganda, not thinking for themselves, not planning for themselves, not even living for themselves.

When people accept the idea that there is no hope for them, that they are born laborers, will die laborers, and that their children are children of laborers and will die laborers, it is easy to indoctrinate them to the point of not thinking, and easy for them to accede willingly to decisions made for them. Then all the information that can be given them is of no avail, because they have not yet developed the capacity for reasoning, thinking, and assimilating.

God's Special Gifts

The greatest gift we have is the gift of life and intelligence, that we are born with the power to think, to feel, to reason, and above all, the power to love. Every child is born with the power to love, as well as with all God's other gifts. The fact that children do not develop more fully in this present age is due to the restrictions and conditioning that are put upon them through age-old beliefs, such as that self-preservation-is-the-first-law-of-nature. But by divine inheritance we do have the gifts of loving, reasoning, thinking. Only as, through the home and the school, we are given the realization of our individual identity and worth, do these inner faculties open and do we begin to assimilate the knowledge that is given us and to understand and see through the deceptions of this world.

When, in addition to the scholastic training that may be given a child, he is instructed in his inner capacities, in the ability to draw forth from within what in religion is called the Word or Truth, but which really means that he lives by virtue of having access to the realm of infinity, a realm of infinite capacity, he learns what "man shall not live by bread alone" means.

Tapping the Infinite Resources Within

Every man who has ever discovered anything, invented anything, or created anything new has had to have the faculty of going back within himself in silence, in quiet, with intense concentration, to draw forth that which heretofore was unknown and which had not been set forth in books. Every creator— whether artistic or literary, or in the area of scientific research— has been led to exercise the faculty of going within himself. Whether or not he knew it, he was tapping infinity; he was tapping the infinite resources which exist within every individual.

If we begin to perceive the nature of God as that infinite, divine consciousness which is the substance, the law, and the activity of all creation, God as spiritual, divine, the all-knowing consciousness, the infinite source of wisdom, life, and love, and then perceive that this is the consciousness of individual man, we then have access to that Infinity through our own consciousness.

A material symbol of that is found in the water faucets in our home. We open the tap, and the water comes through, not because our pipes have any water, but because they have access to the reservoir. But the reservoir has access to the river behind it, the snows or the rains that fall. In other words, every individual tap in our home has access to all the water that is contained in the reservoir and even to the water that is still up in the clouds in the form of rain and snow which will eventually replenish the reservoir.

The Importance of One Individual

So it is that behind what we call our individual capacity is the source of our capacity, and this is infinite. It is because of this that real musicians can bring forth great melodies never before heard, not out of their bodies, not out of their brains, but out of this infinite storehouse which embodies all the music, art, literature, invention, or discovery that ever has been or ever will be known. All these exist in consciousness.

The invention and use of automobiles and airplanes came about because from time immemorial the laws on which these inventions were built have existed. The laws always existed in this infinite consciousness, and along comes an individual who is attuned to that particular facet of life and is, therefore, able to draw forth the laws of automotive engineering or aerodynamics. Another comes along and is attuned to the world of music and draws forth out of this same infinite storehouse or source great music.

This is possible only to an individual who, instead of the common refrain today, "Oh what use is one person!" "What can one little group of people do?" is aware of his identity and of his importance in the scheme of life. Then we cannot help but think of Moses, Jesus, Paul, and John. In a different field, what was the worth of one Edison, one Kettering, one Michelangelo? There are thousands of persons whom we can think of as one individual whose life has borne and will bear fruitage for hundreds of generations. That is how important one life is. So far as we know, no board of directors has ever yet made any great contribution in any field, except perhaps that of limitation or holding back.

It may take two individuals working together, or six working together and cooperating, but each one is an individual, and each must be drawing on the infinite resources of his own being. God is the life of each one; God is the soul of each one; God is the capacity of each one. Man has no capacities of his own; he must draw on the capacities that have always existed within his being.

Drawing Forth the Splendor Within

Having been brought up in New York City in the days of open immigration, when anyone with a five dollar bill in his pocket could be admitted to the United States, it was easy to recognize that these immigrants and the children of these immigrants were often the best students in school. Why? Having been deprived of the right to develop their individual capacities in their homeland, when they came to a free country and found free schools, they almost tore down those schools to absorb all the knowledge in them for their development.

The real nature of our being is God-being. If we are thwarted in bringing that out, if we are held down, or forbidden to develop educationally, artistically, or mechanically, we are being dammed up. Then when the day comes and we can break loose, we are like dry sponges, taking in all the wisdom, the education, and the knowledge that can be given to us.

Probably it is necessary for people to be that hungry for knowledge and wisdom, so that when the opportunity does come, they will avail themselves of it. These people who had been held down and restricted in foreign countries were nevertheless full and complete beings of God, only without the opportunity to develop, assimilate, and demonstrate it.

No one can combat the teaching of the insignificance of being an individual or of the need to unite in order to be strong except through spiritual unfoldment, realization, and the teaching that we are creatures of God, and that in God we are equal. Each one is equal to the full capacity and full measure of Christhood, not that we may attain our full Christhood in any one age, but that that is our goal. How can we rest short of that goal, once we know that as an individual we have within ourselves the capacity of a Moses, a Jesus, or an Edison?

Man cannot live by his outer strength and his outer accomplishments alone. He must eventually come to know that he lives primarily by access to the word of God, the Truth. The truth of religion or the truth about music, art, or mechanics lies within ourselves, and Browning told us that we must open out a way for that imprisoned splendor to escape. But how can we, if we do not first know that we have the infinity of God to draw upon, and that individually our function is to draw it forth in full measure?

Children in school and in the home must be taught their true identity and their true individuality, and the stature of them. Napoleon said that every soldier had a marshal's baton in his knapsack, which is another way of saying this same thing. We have had our measure of great men to prove the worth of what an individual can do and what he should be. No man can live just being a number; no man can live just being a statistic; no man can really live merely being a part of a group. He can associate with groups, but he must not be identified only as a member of a group: he must always be known as an individual with individual, infinite capacity within his own being.

If there were such a thing as one individual or government supporting the rest of us or if there were such a thing as one individual spiritually saving us, we would have a nation of nobodies, going nowhere, accomplishing nothing, living without incentive and without any realization of spiritual identity. Without individual responsibility for our moral and spiritual development, we become automatons.

Moral and Spiritual Development Essential

True education must include something more than how to obtain the material bread of life. It must include the secret of our true identity and of our access to our source. Whatever God is, God is closer to us than our breathing. God appears and expresses individually, so that nowhere on earth is an individual devoid of God, of God-presence, or of God-power. Only when it becomes known and accepted that every individual is an individual unit in the household of God—not only an heir of God, but a joint-heir, so that we are equally heirs to all of the Spirit, which embodies all of the wisdom, all of the good that is within us—do we become truly free.

When we are morally and spiritually developed, so that we do not use the great inventions and discoveries of mankind for evil purposes, we are then in full possession of the right and the ability to draw forth out of consciousness all that exists there. It was a sorrow to Albert Einstein to realize that the secret of the atom, which he had drawn forth from this infinity and which he recognized had such tremendous potential for good, should be used for destructive purposes.

Individually we have the capacity of an Einstein to draw forth all life's secrets. So with our great capacity now for tapping the resources of consciousness in the area of mechanical and medical innovations, is it not clear how important it is that we also tap consciousness for our moral and spiritual development?

Universal Freedom Inevitable

I was born with a particular passion for individual freedom, individual justice, individual rights, and the development of individual capacity. It has been a theme that has run all through my life as far back as I can remember, although not always understanding the why of it. But I do see it now and I do see that all mankind can be enslaved except in proportion as he awakens to the truth of his identity and of his infinite capacity.

The authorities, from the time of Jesus until 300 A.D., were much opposed to the Christian movement. Why? Because it revealed to everyone that he is the son of God; it revealed to everyone that he is important in the scheme of God's universe; it revealed to everyone his innate capacities. Those authorities who seek to rule and dominate the masses cannot succeed with a people thus educated.

There will be freedom; there will be justice; there will be universal freedom, perhaps sooner than we think, because the power of this divine consciousness is unfolding at such a rapid rate. Undoubtedly it broke through in Athens in the earliest days of its democracy, but it had a short life. Ever since the Magna Carta of England, the American Revolution, and the French Revolution the movement toward man's freedom and complete emancipation has been increasing, increasing, and increasing. It has been increasing until now it is sweeping across Africa, not quite in the way we may think it should unfold, nevertheless gaining a foothold. But who can control such movements toward greater freedom after the restrictions that have existed for so long? They may bring much heartache and bloodshed with them, but in the last analysis the result will be the emancipation of the individual, and with that will be the breaking down of the few dominating the many.

Those resisting the movement toward freedom will some day wonder if a steamroller has not rolled over them. There is a steam roller rolling now, and that steamroller is the moral and the spiritual power that is in human consciousness. That is sweeping everything before it as it moves on. The people themselves do not realize what is taking place, and they can do very little to help it because of their lack of understanding. But the spread is so rapid and widespread that even where there are political or ecclesiastical powers that would hold back this divine government, one after another of these is being swept away.

How Progress Can
Become a Universal Blessing

Unless we are told that the kingdom of God is within us, unless we are told that the word of God can be heard within our own consciousness, until we are instructed in the fact that we are as important to God as any individual who ever lived, we will not even make the search within ourselves for the spiritual and moral values that exist there. We will not undertake the search within ourselves for those powers which would make it impossible for anything but freedom to exist on earth.

First we must be instructed and have revealed to us that that which we are seeking is within ourselves, a part of the divine capacities that were given to us in the beginning. But it is we who must learn to draw on these infinite capacities within ourselves. Let us not, however, think to draw on those infinite capacities merely for the purpose of creating art, literature, music, or mechanics. We must draw on these for our moral and spiritual capacities so as to make the artistic, mechanical, and scientific progress of man a universal blessing.

We read in scripture that there is a "He" within us greater than he that is in the world, a "He" that performs that which is given us to do or, using the word, "I" instead of "He," the Master proclaimed, "I will never leave thee, nor forsake thee.[1] . . . I am with you alway, even unto the end of the world."[2] To be instructed in such principles, so that we begin to understand the sacred nature of our being that has within itself divine power and divine grace, can make us free, keep us free, and compel us to assist in bringing freedom to our neighbor. We know that whether it is the African slave in Africa or the slave somewhere else, that individual has the same innate capacity that we have. We yearn that he may be as free as we are to draw upon his innate capacities for life, truth, love, home, freedom, justice, equity, equality.

The Meaning of Grace

To discover this is to discover the secret of the word "grace." None of us has ever done anything to deserve the spirit of God within us. That was given to us as heirs of God. We inherited the spirit of God, this Spirit which is life, love, justice, and freedom, from God, and these were planted within us for a purpose, as a means for our outer expression of free and harmonious living.

Above all things, let us be sure, first, that we ourselves understand and then teach our children and all those who will listen to us that there is an inner grace which will give unto us, and maintain eternally, all good. Our freedom is not given to us of man, but by this inner grace. Justice does not come to us from man, but from an inner grace. Man may be the instrument through which it takes place, but if we look to man, we will not experience it.

By virtue of our infinite individuality, we possess an inner grace, and no man can stand in the way of our individual expression after we have learned of the presence and the power of that grace. The secret that has been hidden from the masses is that we all have within ourselves the power of grace which obviates the necessity of fighting for our rights: "Fear ye not, stand still, and see the salvation of the Lord."[3] There is a power of grace that will ensure us a free and harmonious life, a joyous and abundant life. "I am come that they might have life, and that they might have it more abundantly."[4] This *I* is the spirit of grace, the spirit of God that is within each one of us, and our knowledge and recognition of It is what brings It into expression.

The masses can be ruled, even to their detriment, because they do not know that within themselves is this power of grace, and so they are told, "You are helpless anyhow; you might as well make the best of it." They do not know that all this time God has planted His grace in the midst of them to assure them the good of this life. "I am come that they might have life, and that they might have it more abundantly."

Understanding that we are not living by bread alone reveals that we are living by an inner grace, the word of God, the Christ, or Spirit that is within us. It goes before us to "make the crooked places straight."[5]

Let Grace Be Revealed to the World

Let men know the grace within them, and nobody will ever hold them in bondage. Let men know this, and they will never suffer lack or limitation. Let men know, let them be instructed in the truth that the kingdom of God is within them, and they need not fight. Let them stand still and watch this presence go before them to "make the crooked places straight." Let them stand still, put the finger on the lips, and watch the divine power of God break the shackles from the mind and from the body. Until men are instructed in this truth, they do not have the capacity to think, to assert themselves, to digest, or to assimilate the knowledge that is given them in books.

Grace, the presence and the power of God, is already established in individual man: Jew or Gentile, white or black, it makes no difference. The grace of God is within individual man, and he need only stand still and watch it. Let everyone of us be still and know that *I,* this divine grace, is within, and It will perform whatever is necessary. But we must be still and know. Then something emanates from us, something pours out from us, and it does perform all that is necessary in our experience. It draws unto us everything necessary in our experience. It draws unto us everything necessary for our unfoldment.

"The Lord is on my side; I will not fear:
what can man do unto me?"[6] Why should I fear,
when this grace, this presence sits right there within
me, that which is a rear guard, that which goes before,
that which walks beside, that which is over and above
and under, the blessed spirit of God in man?

We may call it the Buddha-mind if we are walking the Oriental path, the Christ if we are walking the Christian path, or the Messiah if we are walking the Hebrew path. It is all the same. It is divine grace.

Man Shall Not Live by Temporal Power

When we think of the great problems of this world that are facing the administrative leaders of all countries, does it not seem strange that the power rests with half a dozen men in this entire world to make or break the freedom and the peace of the world? Does it not seem strange that with four billion people, half a dozen can decide the issues of war or peace, freedom or slavery? That is the mass hypnotism that would try to make us believe that we are helpless pawns. And it could come true, except that there are enough people on earth realizing every day:

> I need not fear what temporal power can do.
> It is only the "arm of flesh."[7]
> We live under divine grace.

When I say "we," I do not mean some particular religious group. I mean that every individual on the face of the earth has this divine grace, and enough of us know it so that temporal power will crash of its own nothingness in the presence of this divine grace.

Nothing could ever stop the onrush of temporal power except the revealed truth that man shall not live by temporal power, but by the word of God, this inner grace. This it is that will pull down the entire stronghold of temporal power. The scriptural accounts of Samson with his long hair and David with his slingshot are merely symbolical teachings revealing that temporal power always crashes in the presence of a pebble, of a tiny little bit of understanding of a divine grace which is greater than all of these.

TAPE RECORDED EXCERPTS
Prepared by the Editor

This month's letter brings out clearly the significance of grace in the unfoldment of freedom, both individually and collectively. When we learn the meaning of grace and have the experience of grace taking over and living our life, life takes on an inner glow which carries over into our outer experience. Below are excerpts from some of the tape recordings that point up the meaning and function of grace.

The Meaning of Grace

"We have thought heretofore that grace was something you sat around waiting for God to bestow on you. No, no, you don't have to wait for grace; you can move right out from under the law this minute. Just relinquish your desires, and you are under grace. Just relinquish your belief that you need something in the realization that God knows your need before you do, and you are under grace. . . .

"The law of cause and effect is not really a law. It is a belief that concerns a selfhood apart from God. It is a false sense of self which brings itself under the law in this wise: If I say I have to pay next month's rent, I have brought myself under the law. If I say that I and the Father are one and that I do not live by bread alone, I have brought myself under grace."

Joel S. Goldsmith, "Old Testament, New Testament:
The Law, Grace, and Truth,"
The 1956 First Steinway Hall Practitioners' Class, Tape 4:2.

"Grace is fulfillment. The gift of grace, which is of God, does not bring us a partial success, a partial happiness, nor does it bring erroneous nature. . . . Therefore, our studies are all in the direction of bringing us to a place in consciousness in which we can relax, rest in a state of receptivity, and then eventually hear or feel something that would indicate, 'Fear not, it is *I*. Be not afraid, it is *I*. . . . The Christ is functioning through me and as me, and I am standing to one side, as it were, being a beholder of the Christ, Truth, living my life.' "

Joel S. Goldsmith, "Above the Law to Grace,"
The 1963 Kailua Private Class, Tape 1:2.

"Grace is fulfillment. The gift which is of grace, which is of God, does not bring us a partial success, a partial happiness, nor does it demand of us that which we cannot fulfill. Grace brings a task to us, but grace also brings the understanding and the strength and the wisdom to perform it, and grace brings whatever is necessary for fulfillment. . . . Understanding God to be the giver of all good, we do not look to each other even for those things that constitute our human or legal rights. . . . Within the depths of our being, we look to God for our good."

Joel S. Goldsmith, "Grace," *The 1953*
First Portland Class: Self-Completeness in God, Tape 3:1.

"When you reach the place of knowing that life is lived by grace, you will have dropped your human qualities of goodness and badness. . . . Any belief in *your* goodness is just as evil as the belief in *your* badness. Any belief in *your* prosperity is just as evil as the belief in *your* lack, because prosperity is no more yours, than lack is. Prosperity is the gift of God, and there is no lack to those who know that. Lack is the product of the belief that supply is mine or yours or his or hers."

Joel S. Goldsmith, "Above and Beyond the Pairs of Opposites,"
The 1963 Kailua Private Class, Tape 7:2.

"Thy grace is my sufficiency in all things. . . . And where is God's grace? It must fill all space because It cannot be localized in either time or space. Nothing of God can be localized in time or space and there is no time or space where God is not, nor where the allness and fullness of God is not. Therefore, with all thy getting, get God, and all these things will be added unto you. In the presence of God, there is fulfillment."

Joel S. Goldsmith, "Contemplative Meditation on Grace," *The 1960 Los Angeles Closed Class,* Tape 7:1.

Chapter Three

God's Blessing
Is Not Dependent
on Thought or Thing

With my whole heart have I sought thee:
O let me not wander from thy commandments.

Thy word have I hid in mine heart,
that I might not sin against thee.

Blessed art thou, O Lord: teach me thy statutes.

With my lips have I declared all the
judgments of thy mouth.

I have rejoiced in the way of thy testimonies,
as much as in all riches.

I will meditate in thy precepts,
and have respect unto thy ways.

I will delight myself in thy statutes:
I will not forget thy word.

Psalm 119:10-16

We read a great deal about the fact that this is a materialistic age and that we must become more spiritual. But we read very little about what it means to live in a materialistic age and even less about what it means to be spiritual and to live spiritually, and how this is to be accomplished. Yet, above all things, how to live the spiritual life is of paramount importance. What does it mean to live in the word of God? What does the oft repeated statement that we have become too materialistic really mean?

What Does It Mean to Be Materialistic?

From the standpoint of the religious life, to be materialistic means to have too much faith, dependence, and reliance on matter, on external effects, rather than on the inner, invisible, spiritual consciousness. Some even believe that it is quite sinful to use all our modern discoveries, inventions, and comforts. But there is nothing materialistic about modern science or modern inventions except in an utter dependence on these, rather than on the use of them as natural parts of our daily living.

The statement, "The love of money is the root of all evil,"[1] is often misinterpreted. Immediately, there are those who begin to fear money and who think there is some kind of a sin about having it. There is nothing sinful about money, unless it would be our use or misuse of it. Money, in this modern age, and even in ancient days, is a very necessary commodity. Churches have not found a way of dispensing with the use of money. To be materialistic, however, means to place our faith and confidence in money, and look upon it as if money were our supply, which it is not and never can be. Supply is of God, and therefore supply must be spiritual.

It is materialistic to believe that money is supply or that supply is material. It is spiritual to understand that supply is of God and is spiritual, and that money is merely our concept of spiritual supply, a necessary part of our daily living. All the modern conveniences of life are really the product of spiritual laws. They are spiritual laws understood by man and then translated into what we call automobiles, airplanes, refrigerators, ranges, and all the rest of the comforts of modern living.

Asceticism has never solved anyone's problems; asceticism increases problems. Doing without and sacrificing is not the spiritual path of life, but not being *attached* to the things of this world is the spiritual way. Therefore, when we speak of a materialistic age, we are not necessarily referring to the great inventions, discoveries, conveniences, and comforts of life as being erroneous. We are speaking only of the fact that our lives have become so dependent on these that we think our safety, security, happiness, peace, and health are in these. And they are not.

The Meaning of Living Spiritually

To be spiritually minded, to have that "mind. . . which was also in Christ Jesus,"[2] is to understand that "man shall not live by bread alone, but by every word that proceedeth out of the mouth of God."[3] This does not do away with bread, automobiles, airplanes, and the wonders of modern science. This merely means that we do not live by them: we live by the grace of God, by every word of God that we can entertain in our consciousness.

In the Western world, very little thought has been given to living spiritually, even though considerable attention is given to living from a religious standpoint. There is a difference, however, between living a religious life and a spiritual one. On this subject, the Master made it clear that the scribes and the Pharisees were perhaps the most religious of all people of that era. But Jesus said to his disciples, "Except your righteousness shall exceed the righteousness of the scribes and Pharisees, ye shall in no case enter into the kingdom of heaven."[4] How could anyone's righteousness have exceeded their righteousness, when they lived their entire lives in the temple, obeying the laws of the temple, the Ten Commandments, and all of the other commandments given to them by their religious hierarchy? Yet, he said that their righteousness must exceed this obedience to rules, regulations, laws, feasts, fasts, ceremonies, rites, and rituals.

Then the Master revealed to his disciples what he meant by the spiritual life: seeking God, not in holy mountains, holy cities, or holy temples, but within; not sacrifice, but benevolence, not rites, rituals, ceremonies, or creeds, but loving our neighbor as ourself, loving the Lord our God with all our heart, with all our soul, forgiving seventy times seven, taking no thought what we shall eat, what we shall drink, or wherewithal we shall be clothed; but seeking the kingdom of God that is within us.

"If God so loved us, we ought also to love one another."[5] Here we see that spiritual living has to do, not with obedience to rules, but with a code of spiritual conduct. It is a whole new outlook on life, because in living spiritually we are not seeking to obey man, but rather the word of God.

Finding Our Teacher and Teaching

In order to follow the spiritual way of life, it is necessary to know the way and the word of God. So, in this modern age, we are returning to the ancient system of learning a spiritual way of life, which includes finding teachers and teachings that will take us along the spiritual path. Since we are not all constituted alike, since each of us is of an individual state of consciousness, there is no one teacher or one teaching that can ever meet the needs of all mankind.

It becomes necessary for an individual seeking to live by the word of God and the way of God to pray diligently within himself to be guided to his teacher or teaching. This has not been so important in the West in the past. It is important now because the spiritual way of life must be imparted by spiritual means, by the Spirit rather than by a book, by rules, or by laws. It is for this reason, then, that each seeker finds the one teacher with whom he feels a rapport, with whom he feels at one.

Furthermore, at the beginning of our spiritual search, we ourselves are in no position to know what is truth and all that must be known. Therefore, while all truth is demonstrable, in our beginning days we must have enough confidence in our teacher and in the particular teaching we follow to enable us to accept the truth uttered by the teacher.

We will not always find our teacher to be the one who is recommended to us by a friend or the one who is popular at the moment, or even the one who seems to be meeting the needs of someone else. Every seeker should be careful that he earnestly turns within for guidance, because just as in coming to the Master we have to sit at the feet of the Master, so as we find our teacher and our teaching, there must be that feeling of confidence, that feeling of oneness that enables us in the beginning to accept that which is given to us until we ourselves are able to prove and to know for ourselves. When that time comes, the teacher has performed his function, the teacher has fulfilled his mission, and the student is then so consciously one with the Father that the student has in turn become a teacher.

Spiritual Living Involves a Surrender

As we approach the subject of spiritual living in the message of the Infinite Way, we learn that we cannot mold God to our lives, to our wishes, or to our desires. We cannot influence God to do something for us or for anyone else that we may have in mind. We cannot get God to do our will; we cannot influence God to be other than what God is. Spiritual living demands a surrendering of ourselves to the will of God, surrendering our desires, our hopes and ambitions to the will of God so that God will not do *our* will in us, but God will do God's will in us, that we may be the instruments or transparencies through which God's grace reaches all the earth and through which God's will is done on earth.

This requires a tremendous transition in consciousness. It requires a surrender of all our ideas of prayer. It really compels us even to surrender the concepts of God that we have entertained, especially the concept that in some miraculous way and for some miraculous reason, God will do for me and mine what I would like to have done. There is no such God. Instead we must mold ourselves to the will, the way, and the law of God.

Right here we see how important it is to believe that the teacher has experienced this, because it has been said many, many times, "They have taken away my Lord."[6] It was said of old, and it is said now: "You have taken away my hope and confidence in the God I erroneously conceived." Most of our gods are man-made. We have made our own ideas of God, or we have accepted someone else's idea of God, and we do not realize that God is not that way at all.

Because of the Nature of God, Grace Is

One important point in spiritual living which requires a tremendous transition in consciousness is that the blessing of God in our individual experience is not dependent on anything. It is not dependent on our first being good; it is not dependent on our first obeying laws or going through rites or ceremonies. The blessings and grace of God are not dependent on any thoughts we think or on any acts we do or do not do. The blessings and grace of God are free. They are not a reward for studying books; they are not a reward for attending church; they are not a reward for being benevolent or for tithing.

The grace of God and the blessings of God come to us for one reason only and that is that God is omnipresence. God is here where we are, for no reason for which we are responsible. The very nature of God is omnipresence, so we are always in the presence of God, are always being blessed by that presence, and are always receiving the grace of God—not for reason of our own worthiness, only because of God's nature.

God's nature is omnipotent, all-power. So God does not eradicate sin, disease, lack, and death because of anything we do, but by reason of the fact that there is no power to oppose the reign of God. There are many times when we and the world have not benefited by this power. That is because we have separated ourselves from the word of God, from the will of God, and from the way of God by our spiritual ignorance. The very act of looking to God for something is a barrier; the very believing that some act of our own can induce God's blessing is a barrier; the very belief that we can deserve God's good is a barrier. God's grace is not to be bought, not with money, not with some specified mode of human conduct, and not with thinking. God's grace can be realized only through the understanding of Its omnipresence and omnipotence, and as the Master revealed, Its omniscience.

Man Cannot Invoke God's Blessing

"Your heavenly Father knoweth that ye have need of all these things.[7]. . . It is your Father's good pleasure to give you the kingdom."[8] And he did not say after you have read so many pages of a book, or after you have sat in meditation for so long. Why, then, do we read, and why do we meditate? In order that we may receive from those who are a step ahead of us some instruction as to how to avail ourselves of that which is omnipresence, omnipotence, and omniscience.

The entire message of the Infinite Way is built on the revelation of God as being the Way, the Word, and the Life of man, not of man doing something to invoke God's blessing.

It takes weeks, sometimes months, to make our mind behave, to compel our mind to resist the temptation of asking or pleading with God, hoping to satisfy or to please God. There is nothing at all in the kingdom of God or in the spiritual revelation which says that an act of man will bring about the blessing of God. The blessing of God is here where we are, even in a hell that we may have created for ourselves, a hell of sin, a hell of poverty, or a hell of disease. We may be in any or all of these, and yet God is there, and God is available in that moment when we stop taking thought for our health, our supply, or our morals, and accept the fact that God's grace, God's blessings, and God's purity are here where we are and then let these function.

Instead of having to be humanly good to find God's grace, if we center our attention on the realization of God's grace, God's grace will make us good, even in spite of ourselves. Rather than trying to get God to make us healthy, we take no thought for our health for the time being, and realize that the healing nature of God is not dependent on what we do or think, but on the very nature of God Itself. It is God's nature, as revealed by the Master, that we have life, that we have twelve basketsful left over each day to share with those who are not yet aware that God's grace is free.

God's Grace Is Without Price

God's grace is just as free to the Jew as to the Christian, just as free to the Catholic as to the Protestant, just as free to the Taoist as to the Vedantist or Buddhist. In the kingdom of God there is no such thing as a religion, no such thing as a church, except that we ourselves are that church, that temple of the living God. The temple is not in a holy mountain, and it is not in a holy Jerusalem, for "know ye not that ye are the temple of God, and that the Spirit of God dwelleth in you?"[9] We must be able to relax and accept this and realize that we have struggled for what we already possess; that we have wandered around the world in search of the Holy Grail, spending our money, our strength, and wearing out our clothing, seeking for the Holy Grail that is right here where we are, already ours without price. What Isaiah said years ago is just as true today, "Ho, everyone that thirsteth, come ye to the waters, and he that hath no money; come ye, buy, and eat; yea, come, buy wine and milk without money and without price."[10] The grace of God is not dependent on money; it is not dependent on our efforts: it is dependent on our realization of omnipresence; it is dependent on our realization and understanding of the nature of God.

God Awaits Our Turning

We turn away from man-made concepts of God, and turn within that God may reveal Itself to us.

> I am closer to you than breathing.
> I will never leave you, nor forsake you.
> You cannot buy Me; you cannot even displease Me,
> for I am not displeased with My own image
> and likeness, the son of God which you are.

> That part of you which is wandering around
> in the world as a prodigal, I do not even know
> that you are out there; I have no knowledge of what
> you are doing. I have knowledge of you only
> when you turn yourself to Me within you.

> As long as you are not turning yourself within to Me,
> the Me that is within you, the I that I Am,
> I cannot see you in that outer darkness,
> but I am like the father in the scripture
> waiting for your return.

In the moment of your return, the jeweled ring and the robe await you: your spiritual harmony, freedom, health, wealth, and all good. In reality, they never left you; they were never taken from you. God never deprived you of your health and wealth, even in your deepest sins. You deprived yourself by turning away from divine grace, the son of God that was established in you in the beginning.

"For I have no pleasure in the death of him that dieth, saith the Lord God: wherefore turn yourselves, and live ye."[11] Turn again within. Do not take any man's word for this; do it and see if the Master did not speak truly when he uttered, "Before Abraham was, I am.[12]. . . I will never leave thee, nor forsake thee.[13] . . . I am with you alway, even unto the end of the world.[14]. . . I am come that they might have life, and that they might have it more abundantly."[15] *I* am here, omnipresent, here where thou art.

We need no man's word for this. We need only a few weeks of that turning within, giving up all attempts to reach God, and let God announce to us that the kingdom of God is within us. It is not to be bought for money; it is not to be bought. There is no favoritism; there are no teachers who can give us God; there are no teachings that can give us God, for God is not withholding Himself from us, and therefore cannot be given to us. God can be realized where we are.

Then of the human errors that we have accumulated, not only in this life, but in many lives before, we will be purified. The karma that we have built up will be dissolved, because there cannot be evil, not even the past memory of evil, in this presence of God. When we are consciously in the presence of God, we are made whole; we are purified within and without.

We Have Separated Ourselves from God

Our erroneous concepts of God, prayer, and religion have been the very barriers separating us from the grace of God that has been with us "since before Abraham," and that will never leave us, that will be with us to the end of the world. It is all in accepting this truth. If this truth does not bring out in us a feeling that it must be so, it may be that there still will be days, months, or years before us until our readiness for surrender.

In our materiality we have built up within ourselves even a materialistic faith in God, because the very belief that God will do something for us is a materialistic belief. God will not do anything for us; God constitutes our very being. Our realization of this, coupled with the realization of the nature of God changes our lives. Eventually, we come to understand that the nature of God is the nature of our being, and so when the Psalmist tells us to seek the way of God and the word of God, it is only because we have separated ourselves from the way of God and the word of God, and we have sought to gain God's favor. It is not to be gained; it is not to be won; it is already ours as His gift.

The Son of God
Is Present in Us

It is the nature of God that we be free. It is the nature of God that we be whole. God sent His beloved Son to heal the sick, raise the dead, feed the hungry, forgive the sinner, and preach the gospel. The son of God is more than a man who lived two thousand years ago; the son of God is the spirit of God that dwelt in the man Jesus, and that dwells in every man. Therefore, the son of God is present in you and in me. No one had to buy God's grace from Jesus, nor did he instruct his disciples to sell God's favors. His message was to come and enjoy them. They are ours by the grace of God, not by the grace of man, regardless of how holy that man may be. All of God's good is ours by grace as the gift of God.

The part that meditation and a teacher play now, as in the days of the Master, is in the instruction and in the proving. The teacher must not only instruct the student in these truths, but must in some measure show forth and demonstrate the truth as the Master did through his healing works. Then the command to us is, "Go ye and do likewise", and to those who become disciples, "Go out into all the world and preach this gospel, and reveal through healing that God's grace is a gift."

Surrender and Relax from Concern

Let us begin today; let us begin with this very moment to relax and surrender our desires. Let us have no desires in these next few moments, nothing at all in mind that we want God to do for us. It is easier to surrender these desires when we are two or more united together in a very deep spiritual consciousness. It is much easier to do that than when we attempt it alone.

It is for this reason that where two or more are gathered together in this consciousness it is easier to surrender ourselves and to release God. Eventually we find it possible to do it when we are alone in our meditation, and later we can do it even when we are driving the car or when we are at our business or working in our profession.

Release God from all responsibility to you. Drop all concern for the things of this world. Take no thought for your food, for your health, or for your family life. Take no thought for the world's peace; take no thought for the enemy—physical, mental, moral, financial, or political. Have no fear of the enemy, because your assurance is that God's grace is closer than breathing.

The son of God is established within me.
God's peace is upon me.
God's love envelops me,
enfolds me, upholds me;
God's wisdom governs me.

"Whither shall I go from thy spirit?"[16]
Wherever I am, Thou art, wherever Thou art, I am,
for I am in Thee as Thou art in me, for we are one.
Thou knowest the needs of all mankind, and it is
Thy good pleasure to give us the Kingdom.
Thy grace is my sufficiency in all things.
I live, and move, and have my being in

Thy kingdom, Thy grace, Thyself.
Thy grace is not dependent on anything.
Thy grace is not dependent on what I am thinking;
It was here before I knew it, and my thinking has
only made me aware of It.
Thy grace is not dependent on me,
but on Thy very own nature, Thy very own nature
which is grace, love, and wisdom.

My actions or thoughts, even for good,
will not make Thee function, but Thy functioning
will change my thoughts and my deeds.
I surrender to Thee all that is erroneous or evil
in my makeup, and I surrender to Thee
all the good that I think I am,—
all my self-righteousness, along with all desires.
I surrender all fears, for in Thy presence
there is liberty; in Thy presence there is naught
to fear. I shall not fear what mortal circumstances,
conditions, or persons can do to me, for in
Thy presence is freedom from all the ignorant and
destructive beliefs of the world.

God's Will for Man

God is as close to the atheist as He is to the believer, and even as atheistic beliefs or agnostic beliefs cannot separate us from the love of God, neither life nor death can separate us from the love of God, for the love of God is free and omnipresent, not dependent on thing or thought, not dependent on thought or deed. God's grace is free. The healing power, the forgiving power, the supplying power of God is not dependent on taking thought, for "which of you by taking thought can add one cubit unto his stature"[17] or "make one hair white or black"?[18] If we cannot, by taking thought, do the least of these things, how can we by thought disperse that enemy that is without the gate?

The grace of God is not dependent on our doing anything or thinking anything; it is dependent on one thing alone: "And ye shall know the truth, and the truth shall make you free."[19] The truth is:

"I and my Father are one."[20]
Here where I am, God's grace is my sufficiency.
In my physical, mental, moral, financial, and
political life, God's grace is my sufficiency,
not dependent on thing or thought.

The nature of God is the freedom of man; the nature of God is the health of man; the nature of God is the wisdom of man; the nature of God includes man's safety, security, and above all, peace. The nature of God is that we have peace: peace of mind, peace of body, peace in our individual and collective life, peace in our national and international life. It is the will of God that we have peace; it is the nature of God that we have peace and not be afraid of what mortals think or do.

I seek not that God do my will;
I seek only that God's will be done in me.

The Nature of God Makes Meditation Easier

God is not a being that man has to coerce or influence. It is the very nature of God to be the health of our countenance; it is the nature of God to be the purity of our mind and the wisdom of our mind. It is the nature of God to be love.

This now should make our meditation periods easier, because the barrier to successful meditation is always the attempt mentally to reach, to contact, to enlighten, and to inform God; whereas meditation does not have that purpose. Meditation is a relaxing in the awareness of the spiritual nature of God. It is really an inner communion.

> Thank You, Father. Here where I am,
> You are; all that You are, I am;
> all that the Father has is already mine
> by virtue of the nature of God, not by might, not by
> power, but by the very spirit of God. God's grace is
> upon me; God's blessing is upon me.

With that realization, we become still. We are still and know that *I,* the *I* at the center of our being, is the son of God that was sent to us that we might have life, and that we might have it more abundantly.

We do not have to tell this *I* that is within us of our needs or desires, or even of our wanting to be pure. We cannot fool God; we cannot fool the *I* that is within us.

> Just relax! *I* that is within you am come
> that you might have life, and that you might
> have it more abundantly.
> Take no thought for the things of "this world."
> Do your work; fulfill your mission on earth,
> in your household, in your family,
> in your business, in your art, in your profession.
> *I* am the very bread of life, the very supply.
> *I* am here that you might have it more abundantly.

With this meditation we will find a peace descending, and eventually the words will come to an end. Perhaps for twenty, thirty, or forty seconds we will be completely at peace, without a single thought. That is sufficient. That is why it is much better to have six or ten one to two-minute periods every day than it is to have one or two half-hour periods of relaxing into God's grace. We are not seeking anything; we are remembering:

>Thy grace is free. It is not dependent on
>what I think or do; Thy grace is free.
>My remembrance of this will make me think
>and do that which is spiritually right.

It is possible to love this God with all our heart, with all our soul, and with all our might, for this God has no remembrance of the past; this God has full forgiveness in the present.

TAPE RECORDED EXCERPTS
Prepared by the Editor

The listing of the titles of chapters in the writings dealing with Christmas and the recordings used in the preparation of these chapters, proved to be of such inestimable value to the students in gaining a deeper awareness of the real meaning of Christmas that at this Easter season which marks the culmination of the Christ experience, the Easter messages found in Joel S. Goldsmith's writings are listed below.

Those students who work with these chapters and recordings throughout the coming months will have their own special Easter-experience of rising above this world of mental concepts into the realm of pure Consciousness.

The Easter-Experience

"Resurrection," Chapter 4 of *The 1957 Infinite Way Letters* from Joel S. Goldsmith's "The Teacher Within,"
The 1956 Second Steinway Hall Closed Class, Tape 2:2;
"Establishing your Spiritual Integrity,"
The 1955 First Kailua Study Group, Tape 15:1.

"The Secret of the Resurrection," Chapter 3 of *The 1959 Infinite Way Letters* from Joel S. Goldsmith's "The Secret of the Resurrection," *The 1958 London Open Class,* Tape 4:1.

"Transition," Chapter 4 of *Our Spiritual Resources* from Joel S. Goldsmith's "Questions and Answers on the Mystical Life and Healing," *The 1958 Second Chicago Closed Class,* Tape 3:1, and "Tenth Chapter of John, I am Come," *The 1958 London Open Class,* Tape 3:1.

"The Esoteric Meaning of the Easter Week," Chapter 4 of *The Contemplative Life* from Joel S. Goldsmith's "Maundy Thursday, Good Friday, Easter: Esoteric Meaning," *The 1959 Maui Advanced Work,* Tape 3:1.

"Christ Raised from the Tomb," Chapter 4 of *Man Was Not Born to Cry* from Joel S. Goldsmith's "Christ Raised from the Tomb," *The 1961 Hawaiian Village Open Class,* Tape 5:2.

"The Power of Resurrection," Chapter 4 of *Living Now* from Joel S. Goldsmith's "The Principle of Power and Love," *The 1962 Princess Kaiulani Open Class,* Tape 1:1.

"Truth Unveiled," Chapter 4 of *Beyond Words and Thoughts* from Joel S. Goldsmith's "Truth Unveiled." *The 1963 Kailua Private Class,* Tape 3:2, and "From the Metaphysical to the Mystical," *The 1963 Kailua Private Class,* Tape 4:2.

"I am Come," Chapter 3 of *The Mystical I* from Joel S. Goldsmith's "The Unveiling," *The 1963 London Work, Tape* 6:2.

"Easter, a Rising Out of Material Sense," Chapter 3 of *Living Between Two Worlds* from Joel S. Goldsmith's "Between Two Worlds," *The 1964 Oahu/Maui Series,* Tape 3:1, and "The

Power and Function of the Spirit," *The 1964 Oahu/Maui Series,* Tape 2:1.

"This Is Immortality," Chapter 4 of *The Altitude of Prayer* from Joel S. Goldsmith's The Preparation of One Power"; *The 1962 Los Angeles Closed Class,* Tape 2:1, "Immortality," *The 1958 Manchester Closed Class,* Tape 2:1, "Spiritual Discernment Through Meditation Reveals the Kingdom of God," *The 1963 Manchester Work,* Tape 1:2, and "Preparation for Prayer," *The 1962 Chicago Closed Class,* Tape 1:2.

Chapter Four

The True Demonstration

Take no thought for your life, what ye shall eat,
or what ye shall drink; nor yet for your body, what ye
shall put on. . . For your heavenly Father knoweth
that ye have need of all these things. But seek ye first
the kingdom of God, and his righteousness;
and all these things shall be added unto you.
Matthew 6:25,32,33

With many truth-students, the word "demonstration" has become a part of their vocabulary. They have come to believe that they have the right to health, harmony, wholeness, completeness, perfection, and satisfaction as the fruitage of their study. Too often, however, as the student continues in this work, he finds his attention fastened too much on the outer demonstration rather than on what produces the effect, that is, on what brings the demonstration into expression or manifestation.

Basis of "Miracles" of Great Spiritual Leaders

The Hebrews thought that the manna falling from the sky was the demonstration. In fact, they believed it so firmly that they rushed out to gather all the manna they could, not only for what they needed for the day but to store up for tomorrow, not realizing that the manna was not their demonstration. The demonstration was their consciousness of God's presence, the consciousness of the activity of God, the consciousness of God as fulfillment.

Moses' entire demonstration was based on his realization of I Am. It was Moses' realization of I Am which produced the manna falling from the sky. The demonstration really was a realization of I Am: and the result of the demonstration was the manna.

Throughout scripture many miracles such as the multiplication of loaves and fishes are recounted. Did the Master multiply loaves and fishes? No, he said, "I can of mine own self do nothing.[1]. . . The Father that dwelleth in me, he doeth the works."[2] But what is "the Father that dwelleth in me"? He referred to that Father later as the truth which is the Comforter, the spirit of truth,[3] the conscious awareness of truth or the consciousness of the presence of God. Any of these terms is descriptive of the Father within. Thus it was the Master's realization of the Father within that was the demonstration. The result of that awareness was the multiplication of loaves and fishes. So, too, Jesus did not demonstrate gold in the fish's mouth: he demonstrated the realization of God's presence, and the result of that realization was gold appearing in the fish's mouth.

Importance of a
Consciousness of Truth

So it is that whenever there is an outer demonstration, manifestation, or expression of good, there must first of all be a consciousness of truth within. There must be the substance out of which the demonstration is to appear. Manna cannot fall from the sky outside of one's being. Loaves and fishes cannot be multiplied out here in the world. Everything must have its foundation within our consciousness, and the foundation is our consciousness of truth. That constitutes the Father within, the Comforter, the awareness of the Presence, the seeking and the finding of the Kingdom within.

When the Master tells us, "Seek ye first the kingdom of God,"[4] where shall we seek it? We seek it where he said it would be found: within us. And what does the kingdom of God consist of? When we seek it or find it, what do we find within? Is it not the realm of truth, love, life, the consciousness of harmony, wholeness, completeness, and perfection? All this we find within our own being, but as it is found within our own being, it appears outwardly as manifestation.

Achieving Inner Peace, the Demonstration

The Master said, "Peace I leave with you, my peace I give unto you: not as the world giveth, give I unto you."[5] *My* peace, this inner peace, this inner quiet, this inner confidence and strength that *I* give will appear outwardly as the health of body, as peace of soul, peace of mind, and abundance of purse. But in order to have the good on the outer plane, promised by the Master, there must first be that "My peace," that is, spiritual peace. There must be a realization of the kingdom of God within, and this means a consciousness of truth.

When we seek demonstrations on the outer plane, we seek amiss, and it is for this reason that we fail in the demonstration, because there is no such thing as a demonstration on the outer plane without the substance of which that demonstration is formed. That substance is always our inner peace or consciousness of truth. So the demonstration to be made, then, is not a condition on the outer plane; it is really a consciousness of truth on the inner plane.

When the demonstration of achieving an inner peace or an inner consciousness of truth is made, then the manna will appear without: the multiplication of loaves and fishes, the healings, the raising from the dead, the reformations, the "by day in a pillar of a cloud. . . and by night in a pillar of fire"[6]; the cakes"[7]found on the stones right in front of us, the "ravens"[8] bringing food if necessary. All these demonstrations will be made on the outer plane providing, first of all, that the demonstration of "My peace," or the consciousness of truth, has been achieved on the inner plane.

Seek the Inner Demonstration

To students of the Infinite Way, I say this: Stop this eternal round of seeking outer demonstrations. Seek first your inner demonstration, that is, your consciousness or awareness of truth. Build within your being the substance of life, and then life will appear in its outer form.

Our basis for all this is found in the Master's teachings, more especially where he said such things, as "It is written, Man shall not live by bread alone, but by every word that proceedeth out of the mouth of God."[9] The word by which we live means the consciousness or realization of truth. If we had all the bread, the wine, and the water, if we had all the money, houses, and yachts on the outer plane, we still might not be living harmoniously, healthfully, joyously, because we cannot live by these outer things alone. We have to live by every word of God.

Are We Ready to Surrender Our All?

If we were to start out life at this particular time without a dollar, with only the clothing on our backs, and without a roof over our heads, it would be of only a passing moment. It would be of no lasting concern because everyone reading this letter could begin at once with a consciousness of truth, and in three days, that is, in a comparatively short period of time, would be re-established in a home, health, food, clothing, and in all forms of good. Why is that? Because the outer things that we would be deprived of are only the reflections or expressions of the degree of awareness of consciousness, and if those outer forms were destroyed, in three days this consciousness of truth would raise them up again.

That is the experience of every initiate in the spiritual orders of the world, more especially on the inner plane. They begin their career as initiates after having given up everything and everybody. No one, accepted into the inner realms of spiritual truth is ever permitted to bring his possessions with him. Never! As a matter of fact, the first question is, "Are you ready to surrender your all?" Strangely enough, when that question is asked, it refers not only to material possessions; it also refers to our loved ones. Until a surrender is made even of those, there is no entrance into the inner realm of spiritual existence.

That seems harsh but there is a good reason for such a demand. One thing is certain and that is that we must be able to surrender our all and to realize, "Yes, I could be deprived of everything and every person, turned out in this world alone with only this clothing upon me but with the assurance that because I am God-governed, God-maintained, God-sustained, I would not even miss this evening's meal. It would be prepared for me, and breakfast in the morning, even if it had to be what the world called a miracle of cakes being baked on stones or of ravens bringing food."

Unless a person has that complete inner conviction, he has not yet found the kingdom of God, and he is still playing around out in the world with shadows, with effects. That is where the Hebrews were when they strove to gather in the manna, the manna that they didn't have to struggle for because it was coming right down from the sky without might and without power, just by the spirit of God. If that blessing falls from the sky today, why should anyone doubt that it will do so tomorrow, the day after, and the day after that?

The Gift of Grace, Omnipresent

If we have ever received anything by grace, should it not be our conviction that we will have everything by grace and will not have to store up "treasures upon the earth, where moth and rust doth corrupt"?[10] That does not mean that we should squander our possessions or throw them away. Let us be good custodians of them, but never let us believe that our safety, security, or supply is dependent on them. I don't have to remind you how many times through fire, flood, volcano, and war people have found themselves with no possessions. The Belgians and the French in World War I and again the Belgians, the French, the Dutch, and the Germans in World War II found themselves stranded, some out on the road, who had to begin life all over again.

For some of them it was a terrific struggle because it had to be humanly accomplished. It would have been no struggle for those of spiritual vision. As a matter of fact, for those of spiritual vision, there never were hardships, even during those periods. There is much evidence that those of spiritual enlightenment found protection, safety, security, and abundance throughout all these experiences.

A Consciousness of Truth
Results in Outer Forms of Good

The point for us to remember is that all outer demonstrations of supply, health, protection, safety, and security are but the outer evidence of an inner grace, which is not just a fanciful term, but a consciousness and an awareness of truth. To live by bread alone means that we live by food, bank accounts, investments, certain forms of government, jobs, business, savings, and inheritances. We do not live by these outer things alone but by our consciousness of truth, which results in the possession and the use of these outer forms of good.

At some time or other students must begin to realize this

great truth and build this consciousness within themselves so that they do not live by outer forms but by every statement of truth that they understand, realize, and spiritually imbibe. It is not by quotations of truth or by lip service, but by actually living the truth within their own being, actually assimilating and making it a part of their inner being.

Acknowledge God in All Ways

"Trust in the Lord with all thine heart; and lean not unto thine own understanding. In all thy ways acknowledge him, and he shall direct thy paths."[11] An inner consciousness of that truth will result in an outer demonstration of good. "Lean not unto thine own understanding." Through our education, reading, and environment at home and in school, we have built a knowledge of life and how to conduct ourselves. To "lean not unto thine own understanding" is not an injunction to give that up, but not to depend on it.

We acknowledge God and He directs our path. We acknowledge God as the mind of our being and we draw on It for wisdom, guidance, direction, and intelligence. We acknowledge God as the life of our being, and then we draw on that presence within for youth, vitality, strength, and the harmonious functioning of our body. We acknowledge God as the soul of our being out of which comes the purity of our human existence and our integrity, one to another. We acknowledge God as the very substance of our existence, even as the very substance of our body. Then we shall be expressing in every area the harmony of the substance which is God.

"In all thy ways acknowledge" God. If there is a decision to be made, let us acknowledge God as the One who makes the decision, and let God make that decision in us and through us and for us. If there is to be a sale or a purchase, let God determine the advisability of it, the time of it, the place of it, and the amount of it. As we acknowledge Him as the source of our good, this inner wisdom will be reflected in our outer conduct. We will be led to do the right thing at the right time, say the right thing in the right place, even as the Master instructed the disciples: "When they deliver you up, take no thought how or what ye shall speak: for it shall be given you in that same hour what ye shall speak. For it is not ye that speak, but the Spirit of your Father which speaketh in you."[12]

The eleven disciples meeting to elect the twelfth did not waste one moment in electing him. They turned right to God: "Thou, Lord, which knowest the hearts of all men, shew whether of these two thou hast chosen."[13] They let God choose; they acknowledged God as the One who should fill up their ranks. So with us. In all our ways, as we bring this Infinite Invisible into acknowledgment, It is brought into outer expression.

Keep the Mind Stayed on God

"Thou wilt keep him in perfect peace, whose mind is stayed on thee."[14] Instead of keeping our thoughts stayed on the problem, how to get rid of it, how to overcome it, or how to remove it, the perfect treatment is to keep the mind stayed on God. In so doing we are living and moving and having our being in God-consciousness. As we realize God as the very soul and substance of our being, the very fount of all good, omnipresence, omnipotence, and omniscience, the outer demonstration is taken care of by that consciousness of truth.

We cannot make the manna fall and we cannot multiply the loaves and fishes, but if we keep our mind stayed on God, if we live and move and have our being in the conscious awareness of God's presence, then at the moment food should appear, It will. It will make the manna fall; It will multiply loaves and fishes; It will send ravens with the food.

The mistake we have made is in thinking we make the demonstration, instead of realizing it is God that performs these miracles—not man, not the prophets, saints, or seers. The prophets, saints, and seers keep their minds stayed on God. They live and move and have their being in the consciousness of God's presence and power, and that Consciousness brings forth the demonstration.

The Invisible Meat

"In quietness and in confidence shall be your strength."[15] We do not live by bread alone, by vitamins, or by minerals. We do not get the strength of our muscles through what we eat. It is in quietness and confidence that this strength is formed. In other words, *My* peace, this inner peace or spiritual peace, appears outwardly as harmonious form.

Now we come to one of my favorite inner teachings of the Master, in which he reveals, "I have meat to eat that ye know not of."[16] In that one statement can be found the entire secret of the Master's ministry.

> "I have meat to eat that ye know not of." I have an inner substance; I have an inner foundation; I have an inner seed; I have an inner good that the world does not know. The world cannot see it, hear it, taste it, touch it, or smell it. It is the invisible kingdom of God or consciousness of truth.

Were we for any reason to be thrown out on the street at this moment just as we are and permitted to take nothing with us, what would make our demonstration? What, but the awareness that we have this spiritual meat or spiritual substance out of which our tonight's food would appear, out of which our tonight's resting place would appear, our safety and security. Our cloud by day and our pillar of fire by night would come out of our awareness of this meat that the world knows nothing of.

Our consciousness of truth would appear throughout our forty years in the wilderness. Our consciousness of truth would appear outwardly as the multiplication of loaves and fishes just as it did in the three years of the Master's ministry. It would appear outwardly as the ability to walk in and out of danger untouched. It would appear outwardly as every form of safety, security, and healing, even the raising of the dead. What would do this? The meat "that ye know not of," this inner consciousness of truth. With this inner consciousness of truth, we can lose all of the world's goods, and yet this inner consciousness of truth would operate as an activity in our consciousness and appear outwardly as every form necessary to our fulfillment.

The Consciousness of I Am

What is a consciousness of truth? It is all tied up in the word I. "I Am That I Am,"[17] Moses said. And Jesus said, "I am come."[18]. . . I have meat to eat that ye know not of.[18]. . . I am the bread of life.[19] . . . I am the resurrection and the life.[20]. . . I am the way, the truth, and the life."[21] Our awareness, our consciousness that the I at the center of our being is God and not man, our awareness that the I at the center of our being is the great infinite I Am That I Am, goes before us to "make the crooked places straight,"[22] and It will never leave us or forsake us. "Lo, I am with you alway, even unto the end of the world.[23]. . . Before Abraham was, I am."[24]

The consciousness of the truth that we have meat, we have God, we have the great I Am at the center of our being is far greater than knowing that we have a bank account, a home to which to go, or that we have a return ticket home. This realization that I, the I at the center of our being, has come to us in our individual experience that we might find fulfillment in this world, that we might find that the fullness of good is greater than anything in this world. Its function and Its purpose is to express Itself in all forms of good.

Our consciousness of that truth is the meat that the world knows not of. It is the water which when we drink of it we will never thirst again. It is the wine of inspiration. It is the power of resurrection unto our temple, whether the temple of our body, of our home, of our church, of our wealth, or even the temple of our nation. Whatever temple is destroyed will be raised up again, and quickly, through our consciousness of truth.

I Am, *the Ultimate Revelation*

What is the truth? *"I* am come that they might have life, and that they might have it more abundantly.[18]. . . I will never leave you, nor forsake you.[25]. . . Greater is he that is in you than he that is in the world.[26]. . . He performeth the thing that is appointed for me.[27]. . . The Lord will perfect that which concerneth me."[28] The awareness of this truth is meat, wine, water, and bread. Again *I,* the *I* is the bread of life; the *I* is the meat; the *I* is the water; the *I* is the wine. The *I* is the all in all. When Moses realized this truth, he went from being a shepherd on the hills to becoming the leader of the Hebrew people. When Jesus realized that, he went from being a Hebrew rabbi to becoming the founder of Christianity.

The moment we realize the nature of *I* at the center of our being, we are no longer a housewife, a clerk, or a banker. We are then the leader of our religious world. It is not necessary to found a new religion because this is a religion that is as old as time itself. The most ancient of Hindu teachings was based on the one Ego, the one Ego appearing as many, the one God, the one *I Am* appearing as your individual being and mine. It was Moses' revelation; it was King Solomon's revelation; it was Jesus Christ's revelation; and we find it to be John's revelation in the Book of John and in Revelation.

Out of scripture I have chosen only these few passages to serve as a foundation, but there are several hundred similar citations in scripture. There is no reason why we should not spend time bringing them out of the Book into our conscious awareness. We have aids for doing that in the form of Bible concordances in addition to our own knowledge of the Bible. As we bring these statements of spiritual truth into activity in our consciousness, they become the meat and the water and the wine of life.

The Substance of Demonstration

Whenever we find ourselves with a so-called problem, we turn our attention first to the kingdom within and realize:

> Within me is the substance of whatever is to appear
> in the without. Within me is the meat, the bread,
> and the substance of that which is to appear.

Then we will brush aside this more or less universal belief current in metaphysics that demonstrations come about through some kind of miracle or hocus-pocus in the outer world and will come to understand that there are no miracles.

"Through faith we understand that the worlds were framed by the word of God, so that things which are seen were not made of things which do appear."[29] Everything that appears is made of something invisible. The things that are seen are made by things that are not seen, and so there is no magician's demonstration—something coming from nothing. If a demonstration is needed, there must be the substance out of which it is to be evolved, and what is that substance? Our consciousness of truth, our awareness of truth. Some truth may come to us to take into our consciousness and then we let that truth be the substance or foundation of our outer demonstration.

Our Consciousness of Truth
Becomes a Law to Those in Our Consciousness

Many of us have friends, acquaintances, or relatives who are looking to us for help, spiritual guidance, and prayer. They exist right now in our consciousness. They are as much a part of our consciousness, even though they are not visible to us at this moment and may be far away, as someone sitting right in the same room with us. The fact that a mere two feet may be separating a person from us does not make us any closer to him than to our friends or relatives who may be five or five thousand miles away. We exist to each other merely in consciousness, not in time or space. As we embrace our friends and associates in our consciousness, our consciousness of truth and every word of truth that is active in our consciousness becomes a law unto them: a law unto their health, a law unto their supply, and a law unto the harmony of their existence.

The truth that is active in our consciousness is a law unto all whom we embody within our consciousness, since truth is also law or principle. All those we include in our consciousness—friends, and in many cases even enemies—we embrace in our consciousness of love, and this truth is the law of harmony unto their being. Every word of truth that comes from God and becomes alive in our consciousness becomes the activity of truth or the law of harmony unto everyone within our consciousness. It is for this reason that everyone of whom we are thinking consciously or unconsciously is blessed, not by you or me, but by the activity of truth taking place in our consciousness. There is never anything personal about this.

Only God's Thoughts Are Power

Our human good thoughts can no more benefit persons in our consciousness than our human bad thoughts can harm them. They are subject only to the activity of the word of God in our consciousness, and the activity of the word of God in our consciousness is a law unto everybody in our experience. We are not transferring any thoughts to anyone, nor are we sending out or holding thoughts.

In the Infinite Way, we do not hold good thoughts and we

do not send out good thoughts. We, however, become aware of God's thoughts within our own being. We let God's thoughts come and we let them go, but we do not direct them to any person. Healing takes place within us. Any sense of lack or limitation has to be overcome in us. We give it the only power it has. When our sense of the illusion is removed, it collapses into the nothingness it is.

We do not direct the treatment or meditation to anybody or any condition. We overcome within our own self any belief in the reality or power of evil. We realize within our own being the one power, that is, that God alone is power. It is not that God is a power to be used to destroy evil or negative powers, because in the Infinite Way we do not have two powers. We do not have disease to overcome; we do not have sin to heal or sinners to reform. We have only one power. All else exists as mirage, illusion, or false appearance.

We sit in quietness, not thinking of person or condition, just keeping our mind stayed on truth, which is always a realization of God as the only presence and power, and the further realization that any appearance, whether it be sin, false appetite, disease, ignorance, fear, or death, is not power. These have no power to perpetuate themselves; they cannot maintain or sustain themselves because they are only of the substance of mirage, illusion, nothingness. As we realize this truth, our friend, relative, or patient responds to it because the activity of truth in our consciousness governs all those who are in and of our consciousness.

Maintain the Consciousness of God's Presence

The point in our meditation is to keep the mind stayed on God constantly, to maintain the consciousness of truth, which means a recognition of one Power, one Life, one Intelligence, one Soul, one Presence and, then, not to forget to include the other part, the nothingness of any so-called claim or appearance in the realization that what appears as sin, disease, death, lack, or fear is without power, cannot maintain itself, cannot perpetuate itself, and cannot stand a moment in the presence of this truth of God's allness.

God's allness is really the sum and substance of the Christ-ministry. Even to Pilate's claim to power, Jesus answered: "Thou couldest have no power at all against me, except it were given thee from above."[30] So, to any form of discord or inharmony we, too, may say, "Thou couldest have no power over me unless it came from the Father within. Therefore, I can't even try to take time getting rid of you or overcoming you or praying you away. I have enough to do to stand fast in the realization of your nothingness because of God's allness."

As the world crowds in upon us, in our meditation let us realize that all those who have turned to us for help, for prayer, for comfort, consolation, relief, or freedom are now met together in one place in one consciousness: our consciousness of truth. This consciousness of truth becomes active as a law of harmony unto their being, and it becomes active as a law of elimination to every belief, every appearance, and every mirage. The light of truth in our consciousness illumines this scene so that we behold it as it is, perfect in His image and likeness, dispelling the illusions of sense and the darkness of materiality. The light of truth in our consciousness, which is the consciousness of truth, does that. You don't; I don't.

> "I can of mine own self do nothing," but the con-
> sciousness of truth within me is the law of harmony.
> It is the law of life that illumines this entire scene.

If we try to build demonstrations on the outer plane, we may succeed for a season, but it will not last. It never does in the human picture. "Except the Lord build the house, they labor in vain that build it,"[31] except the consciousness of truth becomes the substance of our demonstration, we shall labor in vain. As we realize this truth, we then become quiet, with ears open and alert in a state of receptivity as if we were actually listening for the voice of God. We let ourselves be still and then comes that inner awareness, that sense of release, "It is so. Thank You, Father; it is done."

Tape Recorded Excerpts
Prepared by the Editor

In a period when the world faces serious economic problems—mounting inflation, growing unemployment, a fluctuating stock market, and an energy crisis—the problem of supply looms on the horizons as a Goliath of tremendous proportions. To the materialistic state of consciousness, money, stocks, bonds, and jobs are thought to be supply, and these are always limited. The truth is that Infinity is the measure of our supply. We come into that awareness as we recognize the spiritual nature of supply as consciousness and, therefore, *already* within us.

The excerpts from the recordings underscore the principles of supply: supply is outgo because it is invisible, omnipresent consciousness.

"Limitation or Infinity?"

"It is not difficult to lose one's fear of lack when it is realized that it is not money that constitutes abundance. But the realization of the ever presence of abundance produces the forms of supply. . . . Do not believe that borrowing money and saying a prayer is a good way to demonstrate supply. . . . Choose ye this day, and come, in meditation and in contemplation to that point where you attain the realization that it is the Invisible, which is ever present where you are, that is to act upon the visible things of your life."

Joel S. Goldsmith, "Transparency for God,"
The 1958 First Maui Lectures, Tape 1:2.

"There is no such thing as a metaphysical treatment that ever can be effective for supply, because supply is not demonstrated through treatment. Supply is demonstrated through a way of life. . . . In material living, supply is getting, but not in spiritual living. In spiritual living, the demonstration of supply is giving. . . . The infinity of supply is at the center of your being. Nothing can be added to you and nothing can be taken from you. It is a continuous outpouring of the infinity of God. . . . No, supply cannot be demonstrated: only the realization of God can be demonstrated, and then let the supply flow."

Joel S. Goldsmith, "Infinite Way Treatment (concluded)," *The 1954 First Honolulu Lecture Series*, Tape 6:1.

"Only the bread that we cast on the water is the bread that comes back to us. . . *I* am the bread; *I* am the wine, *I* am the water. This spiritual truth is the bread that we release and that comes back to us. . . . We do this in the form of what we call treatment or prayer, during that period of communion each day in which we know the truth about this universe and about our neighbor. It is in that period that we forgive our debtors, forgive those who trespass against us, forgive enemies, and pray for our enemies. . . . We turn loose upon the waters of life all the truth that we can bring to conscious remembrance."

Joel S. Goldsmith, "Cosmic Law (beginning)," The 1954 First Honolulu Lecture Series, Tape 13:2.

"You don't need to get integrity: you have it; you are not utilizing it. Everyone has integrity. . . . Just so, we have all the necessary prosperity. We have all the necessary health and wealth, but we are not drawing on it. We are not letting it flow out from us. We are sitting here as if we really were material, limited, finite beings, waiting for our good to come to us and find that it never comes. . . . Start with whatever you have; pour it out; share it; give it; get rid of it; show that your faith is not in it. . . . There is no better way for you to find your spiritual prosperity than to give up that personal sense of selfhood that says, 'I need.'"

Joel S. Goldsmith, "Substance of Prosperity,"
The 1951 Second Portland Series, Tape 2:1.

Chapter Five

God, the Substance of Universal Being

Jesus' statement, "I and my Father are one,"[1] must be ingrained in your hearts and minds as one truth never to be forgotten. Otherwise, you will have a God separate and apart from your own being, and you will be attempting to contact It, trying to be worthy of It, or praying to It. In the Infinite Way you begin your real unfoldment when you can understand not only that God is life, but that God is your individual life. Unless you understand that, you will always be meditating to get health, whereas the life which is God needs no healing. The life which is God can never age or change.

One Individual Mind and Consciousness

All the error, all the mistakes, all your ills come from the ancient belief that there is God *and* man, that there is God, eternal life, *and* your life. The only reason a person has mental upsets or a nervous disease is because of the universal belief that God is mind but that man has a mind separate and apart from God. The mind of God is indivisible and is a facet or instrument of the God-consciousness you are. Understanding that, your mind and mine would continuously show forth the glory of infinite intelligence.

If you accept the universal, world belief that there is a God somewhere to be reached, to be prayed to, or to become at-one with, you lose your demonstration.

> I and the Father are one.
> I and the Father have been one
> "since before Abraham was."[2]
> I and the Father will be one until eternity.
> I and the Father are one, now, always,
> and throughout all time.

Whatever there is of treatment or prayer in our work is the realization of the truth of that *I Am-ness*. To forget that would be to lose the entire sense of spiritual demonstration because it would leave you in a state of having to achieve that oneness or attain it; whereas it is already the truth.

Your World, an Expression of Your State of Consciousness

God is the substance of which this universe is formed, but when you understand that God is your consciousness, does it not even mean something more to realize that God made this universe out of consciousness, your and my individual consciousness, because there is only one? Our consciousness is the substance, the law, and the activity of our universe, not a God-mind or God-consciousness here, not a God-substance seven thousand years ago, but the mind of you, the consciousness of you is the substance, the law, the cause, and the activity of your world, that is, of your experience.

Your world is an expression of your consciousness. If you understand that God is your consciousness, your world is a spiritual world: harmonious, perfect, and complete. If you believe that you have a human consciousness and a human mind, made up of your ancestral beliefs, your home environment, your education or lack of it, then your world becomes a world of finiteness, lack, limitation, sin, disease, and ultimately one of age and death.

The whole question you must determine through your study is: Is God my consciousness or have I a personal, mortal, material consciousness out of which my world of limitation is formed? If you have a personal mind of your own and there is some kind of error in it that would destroy you, sooner or later it is bound to catch up with you.

The Fruitage of the Belief of a Mind and Consciousness Separate from God

The truth is, there is no error in your consciousness. There is not a sign or a trace of sin, disease, or lack in your consciousness, because God is the only consciousness there is. God is the only consciousness that man has, and mind is its instrument. Therefore, the only expression that can come forth from it is infinite good. Some of you will say, "Oh, but look at this world of lack and limitation, sin and disease." Yes, look at it, and you will see the fruitage of the belief that you have a separate mind, will, and consciousness of your own.

This work does not take a Pollyanna attitude; it is not saying, "There is no evil," where there is the appearance of evil. It is declaring that God is universal mind and universal consciousness, and if God is universal mind and consciousness, that means infinite mind and consciousness. There cannot be anything wrong with the infinite, eternal, immortal Consciousness which is God, nor can there be two. Otherwise there would not be infinity, eternality, or immortality. You either have God or you have no God. You either have God as the one Consciousness which makes it your individual consciousness, or you have God as less than infinity.

Metaphysical practice for a century has shown that there is God and that the nature of God is soul or consciousness, infinite. Therefore, it is individual and it is yours and mine. Prayer is not trying to make the sick well or the bad good: it is the recognition of God as the nature and character of individual life. It is the recognition of God as the soul of all being.

The Demand Is
Always Upon the Christ

When the Son of man shall come in his glory,
and all the holy angels with him,
then shall he sit upon the throne of his glory:

And before him
shall be gathered all nations:
and he shall separate them one from another,
as a shepherd divideth his sheep from the goats:

And he shall set the sheep on his right hand,
but the goats on the left.

Then shall the King say unto them
on his right hand,
Come, ye blessed of my Father,
inherit the kingdom prepared for you
from the foundation of the world:

For I was an hungred, and ye gave me meat:
I was thirsty, and ye gave me drink:
I was a stranger, and ye took me in:

Naked, and ye clothed me:
I was sick, and ye visited me:

I was in prison, and ye came unto me.
Then shall the righteous answer him,
saying, Lord, when saw we thee an hungred,
and fed thee? Or thirsty, and gave thee drink?

When saw we thee a stranger, and took thee in?
Or naked, and clothed thee?
Or when saw we thee sick,
or in prison, and came unto thee?

And the King shall answer and say unto them,
Verily I say unto you, Inasmuch as ye have done it
unto one of the least of these my brethren,
ye have done it unto me.

Matthew 25:31-40

There is that oneness pointed out again. "Inasmuch as ye have done it unto one of the least of these,"—you and me, it has been done unto the Christ. Because we are one with the Father, whatever is done unto you or unto me is done unto the Christ. If financial demands are made upon you greater than what you believe you can afford, greater than what you believe you have on hand, as long as you accept the universal belief that there is a you separate from God you will also accept the belief that you have a health and a wealth separate and apart from God. In that degree you will have accepted limitation.

If you make a legitimate demand on me for more money than I have, my answer must be that I do not have it, that it is beyond my means. That is a selfhood apart from God talking. But if I say to myself, "Certainly, I of my own self can do nothing. That which we call this separate entity, this selfhood apart from God, cannot meet this thing, never could, and probably never will be able to. But that's not my true identity. Christ is my true identity. 'I live; yet not I, but Christ liveth in me.'³ This is not a demand made upon me as a person: this is a demand made upon me as the Christ, on the Christ of me."

Somebody may have just telephoned with a case of cancer, another with a case of tuberculosis, and still another with an automobile smash-up, and they ask you to take care of it right away. Inwardly must come the answer, "I can of mine own self do nothing."[4] Nobody expects that you or I individually or collectively can heal anybody or anything, much less so the cancers or consumptions of the world. So what is that demand made upon? Is it made upon Jesus? Is it made upon Joel? Is it made upon you? Or is it made upon the Christ of your being and my being? None of you would be surprised if a healing of any nature took place at once. You would say, "That's natural. The Christ always is the healer, and It does the work." That is the truth.   .

Awake to Your Christhood!

What is the difference between the request to heal a cancer, consumption, paralysis, or a request for a thousand dollars? "Man, whose breath is in his nostrils"[5] cannot meet it, but the Christ can, and the Christ is your true identity. "I live; yet not I, but Christ liveth in me." That is true of me; it is true of you. The only reason you are reading this letter is not to make that come true, but to awaken you to your true identity as the Christ. Awake! Awake! Awake! The Christ will awaken you from this sleep. Open up and realize that the Christ is your true identity, not mortality, not humanness, not limitation.

The Christ is your real being. Awake; awake; awake; and the Christ will give you light. Light as to what? As to your true identity. The Christ is your true identity, so if someone should ask you for a healing, there is no reason to refuse to accept the responsibility because it is not a man or woman who is being called upon. It is your God-ordained being, your real Selfhood, the son of God of you, that which is made in the image and likeness of God and which has been empowered from on High. God gave man dominion over everything, so there is no reason why anyone should not say to you, "Heal me." Inwardly your response would be, "While I can of mine own self do nothing and while my human understanding is too little, the Christ of me can take care of it."

Christ-Realization
Meets Every Demand

Whether you are called upon for healing work or whether the members of your family or those who make a legitimate call upon you for help should suddenly descend upon you asking for more than you think you can do, do not turn away and refuse it. If it is a *legitimate* demand and not just a catering to the carnal mind, take the responsibility as a student of the Infinite Way to realize that even though you humanly see no way to meet it, the Christ of you is infinite, eternal, and It can meet it. Inasmuch as any good has ever been done to you or to me, and you know how much good has been done to you and I can tell how much has been done to me, it was not done unto you or me but unto the Christ, for the Christ is our identity. Every time you meet a need of anyone for love, cooperation, money, supply, a favor, a healing, you are not doing it for him as a human being: you are doing it unto the Christ and through the Christ of your own being.

No wonder Peter and John could turn to the Hebrews and say, "Ye men of Israel, why marvel ye at this? Or why look ye so earnestly on us, as though by our own power of holiness we had made this man to walk?"[6] as if they of their own selves had done it, as if they through their power or understanding had done it. No, it was "the God of Abraham, and of Isaac, and of Jacob"[7] that raised this man up.

So when any call is made upon you, unless you believe that the God of Abraham, the God of Isaac, and the God of Jacob can do it through you, you are not acknowledging that God is your Father and my Father, "our Father which art in heaven."[8] Do you believe that "if the Spirit of him that raised up Jesus from the dead dwell in you, he that raised up Christ from the dead shall also quicken your mortal bodies by his Spirit that dwelleth in you"[9]?

There is no Spirit out here. The Spirit that raised up Jesus from the dead was the spirit of God in Jesus. There is no spirit of God out here that is going to raise you up. The spirit of God that is going to raise you up is the spirit of God appearing through your practitioner, your teacher, your leader, and ultimately when you do the healing work or supplying work, it is going to be the spirit of God through you. It is the activity of the spirit of God, the spirit of Truth in you, that is going to do it.

When are you going to accept your responsibility and understand that this demand is not made upon you? This demand is made upon the Christ of you. Then, when you help someone, you are demonstrating that you are not really helping the person who, as a matter of fact, may get far less benefit from what you do for him than you receive. The person may not even get a lasting benefit from what you do, but you will, because you have demonstrated to your own satisfaction that the God of Abraham, Isaac, and Jacob, the same Spirit that raised up Jesus from the dead is at work here and now in you.

Purpose of Prayer and Meditation

Until you come to the realization that the same Spirit that raised up Jesus Christ from the dead is your very own soul, your very own life, your very own mind, you will be trying to reach It out here somewhere through prayer or through meditation. Prayer and meditation are not for the purpose of reaching some God somewhere, but for the purpose of communion with God. Where is God? The kingdom of God is within you, so the purpose of meditation is not getting at-one with God, it is not seeking God, it is not trying to be worthy of God. The purpose of meditation and prayer is communion with the Father within you.

Prayer is not something that you do. Prayer is something you become aware of within yourself and that God does. You do not pray: you become aware of God praying in you; you become aware of the word of God. The word of God does not come from you: the word of God comes from God *to* you. Therefore, the purpose of your prayer is to develop a state of receptivity in which you can become aware of, hear, if necessary, the "still small voice"[10] within your own being, letting it impart itself to you.

It is not what you say to God that is of any importance. There is no God interested in what you say. What is important is what you hear from God. What impartation do you receive from the Father within? Why do you think the Master went away for forty days at a time? Surely, not to talk to God. God is the infinite all-knowing intelligence, and It does not need conversation. It does not need any help from you or any guidance in telling you what you want or what you think you need. That is disrespect to the all-knowing Wisdom. That is a lack of understanding of the nature of the All-knowing. The Master said, "Your Father knoweth that ye have need of these things. . . . for it is the Father's good pleasure to give you the kingdom."[11]

You do not have to tell the Father what things you need. You have to listen to the Father that the Father may impart infinite wisdom, infinite intelligence, and infinite guidance. From where? From some outside place? No, "the kingdom of God is within you."[12] It is at the center of your being, of your consciousness, and you develop an awareness of It.

When Jesus said that he was "an hungred, and ye gave me meat. . . thirsty, and ye gave me drink. . . a stranger, and ye took me in . . . naked, and ye clothed me. . . sick, and ye visited me. . . in prison, and ye came unto me," was he not describing the lot of human beings? Are they not all either sick, in prison, naked, hungry, or in trouble of some kind? Certainly, that is the continuous state of humanity.

But *ye* gave me meat, *ye* gave me drink, *ye* fed me, *ye* clothed me, *ye* gave me comfort. Where does such comfort come from except from the center of your being, divine Consciousness? Is there any way to feed a man except to feed him with that meat that the world knows not of? Is there any way really to satisfy a person's thirst with a glass of water, or must he not slake that thirst with the waters of eternal life, spiritual inspiration, and spiritual illumination? That is the food; that is the drink; that is the clothing, the white robe of the Christ.

Real Consolation and Comfort

If a person is hungry, it is right to give him a meal, or if he lacks clothing to give him an overcoat or a suit, but that is not the real food and that is not the real clothing. To go to a prison on visitor's day and sit with a prisoner for a half hour is not the real comfort. But when you bring a person the spirit of truth, the meat that the world knows not of, the water which when you drink of it you never thirst again, water that springs up into life eternal, when you give him the white robe of spiritual truth of which the Master spoke, "I will pray the Father, and he shall give you another Comforter. . . even the Spirit of truth,"[13] that is the real consolation to bring to people.

No matter how beautiful they may be, words are very cold comfort on occasions of so-called death or passing on. Mere words leave people comfortless. Only when you have an actual consciousness of the love that feeds and supplies them, with a Comforter in place of what they believe they have lost, do you leave them satisfied, contented, and at peace. Ministering to those who mourn comes out of the depths of the Spirit, not through words, but with your consciousness of God as eternal life. If you visit a person who has had a severe loss and you entertain in your consciousness the truth that God is the only life, that no life can come and no life can go on, that life is eternal and immortal, without having uttered one single word, you can see on the face of that person the comfort that you have given to him. The Infinite Way is a spiritual ministry, and it is the function of those who live the Infinite Way to give people the meat, the wine, the water, the bread, the comfort, the consolation, and the freedom to those who are prison-bound. But there is only one way in which that can be done:

> The kingdom of God is within me,
> the Christ, the I that I really am.
> That soul at the center of my being
> feeds, clothes, sustains, and becomes
> the Comforter unto all who want.

It must come from the center of your being and it must come as the spirit of truth, the spirit of wholeness or holiness.

Spiritual Recognition

When you observe and accept lack or limitation in friends or relatives, you are helping to produce in them a sense of lack or limitation. When you behold wholeness, completeness, and perfection in them, you are bestowing those qualities upon them. That is the only way in which you can give meat, wine, and water. The only way you can give inspiration, food, raiment, freedom, peace of mind, and peace of soul is by beholding God as their innate perfection, God as their real soul, substance, and life.

When you look at any individual and behold God as the reality of his being, you are giving him wholeness, completeness, and perfection, not that he does not have it, but you are bringing it out into manifestation. It is very much like the photograph that has been taken on film. Nothing is visible until the film is saturated with the right mixture of chemicals. Then when you look at it, the image is there in plain view. The truth is that it was there all the time but it was not to be seen until certain chemicals brought it out.

So wholeness, harmony, perfection, joy, peace, power, eternal life, immortality, and all good exist in this room, but they are invisible until someone who is consciously one with God sees with that spiritual perfection that can recognize only the Holy Ghost, the son of God, the divine expression. Such a person knows only the Christ as the Son, the Christ as the Holy Ghost, the Christ as the Father, the Son, the Holy Ghost, all one. All he knows is the spirit of God among men, and then when he beholds that, this invisible picture is brought out into visibility, and someone is healed, comforted, uplifted, improved, or the pain has stopped. What happened? The perfection was always there, but one with God was the majority that beheld even that which was invisible.

Every time you behold any form of discord or inharmony and remind yourself, "Yes, with my eyes, that is the appearance, but I know the invisible picture there, the invisible Christ. I behold there the real soul of that individual, the real strength of his being and body," you have given meat in *My* name. You have given wine and water and raiment and freedom from the prison house. You have fulfilled Isaiah:

> Behold my servant,
> whom I uphold; mine elect,
> in whom my soul delighteth;
> I have put my spirit upon him:
> he shall bring forth judgment to the Gentiles.

> He shall not cry, nor lift up, nor cause his voice
> to be heard in the street.

> A bruised reed shall he not break,
> and the smoking flax shall he not quench:
> he shall bring forth judgment into truth.

He shall not fail nor be discouraged,
till he have set judgment in the earth:
and the isles shall wait for his law.

Thus saith God the Lord,
he that created the heavens, and stretched them out;
he that spread forth the earth,
and that which cometh out of it;
he that giveth breath unto the people upon it,
and spirit to them that walk therein:

I the Lord have called thee in righteousness,
and will hold thine hand, and will keep thee,
and give thee for a covenant of the people,
for a light of the Gentiles;

To open the blind eyes, to bring out
the prisoners from the prison, and them that sit
in darkness out of the prison house.

I am the Lord: that is my name:
and my glory will I not give to another,
neither my praise to graven images.

Behold, the former things are come to pass,
and new things do I declare:
before they spring forth I tell you of them.

Isaiah 42:1-9

Surely God has put His Spirit upon you that you are in truth the children of God. Many of the four billion on the face of the earth have either forgotten that truth or have not even been told about it by their religious leaders. They sit in darkness believing that they are worms in the dust, unfit to touch that holy robe; whereas the truth, found in the scriptures of all people is: *I,* God, have put *My* spirit upon you and you are *My* children. It takes one—a Moses, an Elijah, a Jesus, a John, a Paul— to realize:

> The Lord God has put His Spirit upon me.
> I am not living my own life.
> The Christ lives my life;
> the Christ is my soul;
> the Christ is the supplier,
> the multiplier of the loaves and fishes.
> The Christ is that activity of my own consciousness
> which makes manna fall from the sky,
> which raises even the dead.
> The Spirit of the Lord God is upon me.

When the Spirit of the Lord Is Upon You

With someone who is in discomfort, someone who is in the prison house of darkness or in the prison house of sin, disease, lack, and limitation, instead of pitying that person, turn from the appearance and silently realize:

> I, the Lord, have put My Spirit upon you,
> and you are My children.
> Rise, pick up your bed and walk.
> What did hinder you?
> Is there a power apart from Me?

There is no power apart from God. Stop worshiping germs and any form of destructive influence, and recognize that in and of themselves they never had power, because the spirit of the Lord God is upon you and what can oppose that? Every time you recognize the nonpower of the appearance, you are fulfilling Matthew, chapter 25. You are giving meat to the hungry, water to the thirsty, consolation, freedom, healing, and even raising from the dead. That entitles you to be one of those who sits on the right hand of God which means that it entitles you to come into the realization of your true identity and enjoy the fruits of the Spirit.

Nobody is actually going to sit on the right hand of God; nobody is going to sit on the left hand of God; and nobody is going to be cast into outer darkness. Sad it is that most persons hold themselves in outer darkness by not knowing their true identity; sad it is that they throw themselves outside the kingdom of heaven by their inability to feed the hungry, give drink to the thirsty and healing to the sick. The only reason you do not have that power is the lack of recognition of the truth that the spirit of God is upon you and that the spirit of God is upon them. Such work is possible with the recognition of your true identity and the true identity of all men and women, and in no other way.

After having done some healing work, the disciples came back happy and overjoyed "saying, Lord, even the devils are subject unto us through thy name."[14] What a rebuke they received! "Notwithstanding in this rejoice not that the spirits are subject unto you; but rather rejoice, because your names are written in heaven."[15] There is nothing subject unto you. You have no power over any discordant condition because God is really the only power, and He never made anything of a discordant nature. Just be glad "your names are written in heaven," just be glad that the spirit of God is upon you and upon all men and that, therefore, in reality there are no discords, no diseases, no sins. Those are only appearances that would fool the elect.

Stop this nonsense of believing that you are a good practitioner and you can heal disease. There never was a good practitioner in all the history of the world except the practitioner who knew he couldn't heal disease. The good practitioner is the practitioner who knows that God is the only creative principle of this universe, and God never created anything to heal or reform or enrich. The spirit of God is upon you, and you can drop this illusory sense of a selfhood apart from God.

The Journey from
Genesis to Revelation

If you accept the belief that there is a selfhood apart from God, then you may have to go through the forty years of wilderness-experience with Moses and, while it may be of forty years duration, it might take four hundred. If you accept a God or mind separate and apart from your own, you will be wandering with the Hebrews all the way from Genesis to Malachi. Yes, you will wander through all those books before you ever get into the New Testament, and you may wander through as many countries as they wandered.

There is only one reason for those wanderings, because they all could have ended in the first chapter of Genesis, that is, they might never have started. There never need have been a second chapter of Genesis had the truth of the first chapter of Genesis been realized and dwelt on. God made this world, including man, in his own image and likeness and everything was perfect. Anything God did not make was not made.

If we never had wandered away from the first chapter of Genesis, we would not have needed the metaphysical religions of today, nor the Master as the way-shower. We would all have been at peace. But having strayed out of the first chapter of Genesis, it now appears that we have to take the whole journey up to Revelation. That is a long one. After you come to the New Testament, however, your journey is shorter! The New Testament is the shortest part of the Bible because the distance from the ministry of Jesus Christ to the revelation or realization of "an house not made with hands, eternal in the heavens"[16] is a much shorter journey than the first one. So be grateful that you are in the New Testament heading for Revelation.

Oneness of Consciousness

A healing contemplative meditation is your realization of God as your individual being. The realization of the presence of God in you is the demonstrator of all outward effects. You cannot manipulate the outer scene to produce healings or supply. You can only stay at the center of your being realizing God as your true nature and letting that truth do all the work in what is called the outer plane.

All those who reach out to you for help or are in any way a part of your consciousness—your patients, your students, members of your family, your enemies—all exist within your consciousness. Realize that they all live, move, and have their being in the divine consciousness which is your consciousness of truth. They have brought themselves to your consciousness because they have turned to the Father within for help, for healing, regeneration, spiritual uplift, that spiritual meat and spiritual drink. For that reason the activity of truth in your consciousness now becomes the law unto their being, unto their body, their health, and their affairs.

Spiritual Bread, the Real Demonstration

Effectual prayer is keeping your mind stayed on God and letting the activity of God in your consciousness do everything necessary in the way of demonstration out here. Let me remind you once again that the mistake of the Hebrews was in thinking the falling manna was the demonstration. It was not. Moses' consciousness of the presence of God was the real demonstration, and the falling manna was the result of the demonstration. The multitudes who were with Jesus and who had to be rebuked thought that the multiplication of the loaves and fishes was the demonstration. It was not. It was Jesus' realization of the presence of the Father within him that was the demonstration, and through that demonstration the loaves and fishes were multiplied and that was the result of the demonstration. Keep your mind stayed on this truth:

> God and I are one.
> The mind of God is my mind; the life of God is my
> life; the soul of God is my soul;
> the spirit of God is my spirit.
> The Christ is the true life of my being.
> That truth entertained in my consciousness
> becomes the law of the multiplication of loaves
> and fishes or the healing or raising of the dead.
> This truth of oneness in my consciousness becomes
> the law of harmony unto my universe.

As you seek what we call demonstration for yourself or for others, please remember the nature of the demonstration you are to seek. You are not to seek outer meat, wine, or water. You are to seek the demonstration of spiritual meat, which the Master referred to when he said, "I have meat to eat that ye know not of."[17] You are to seek the demonstration of spiritual water, the water that if you drink of it springs up into life eternal. You are to seek the demonstration of spiritual wine, not the wine from grapes, but the wine of inspiration that results outwardly, in harmony, wholeness, completeness, comfort.

Pray for the recognition and realization of the bread of life, of the spiritual meat the world knows not, for spiritual water, the water of eternal life. Pray for the realization of that which is to raise up the temple of your body, the temple of your business, the temple of your finances, the temple of your church, the temple of your nation if necessary. Pray for spiritual light, spiritual illumination, and spiritual freedom. As you achieve the realization of that, be assured it will appear outwardly as wholeness, harmony, and completeness.

TAPE RECORDED EXCERPTS
Prepared by the Editor

Nuggets

"Human sense will always be in need of something. That is what constitutes humanhood. But wherever the need is, there is fulfillment because fulfillment exists in the consciousness, really as the consciousness, of individual being because it exists as God. This requires a specific transition in your own consciousness. You may have to meditate days, weeks, and months before you actually come to the realization:

Never again can I have a need, a want, a desire,
but that it will be instantly or timely fulfilled
from within me, without looking out
to a benevolent government, a benevolent parent,
a benevolent relative, a benevolent job,
or a benevolent investment.
No, it will come from the fulfillment
of my consciousness. God is my consciousness.
Therefore, God fulfills Itself daily, hourly, minutely,
in every form necessary.

"But if you do not rise to the realization of God as individual being, you have no foundation. When individuals come to you for help—physical, mental, moral, or financial, how could you give it if you did not have the realization that God is their individual being?"

Joel S. Goldsmith, "Christ Realized Is the Harmony of Being," *The First Kailua Study Group, Tape 11:2.*

Chapter Six

The Substance of All Good

There is no possibility of attaining anything separate and apart from the substance of which it is formed. All attempts to produce anything in the outer realm without achieving the substance of the form must result in failure. So there is no abundance or prosperity to be achieved apart from the substance of abundance or prosperity. In all God's kingdom there is no such thing as demonstrating anything in the realm of effect.

The only demonstration that can be made is in the realm of cause, and then that cause appears as effect. Home, supply, and transportation are effects of the one infinite substance, without which substance there could be no effect. The demonstration must begin within our own being, and that demonstration must take the form of achieving, acquiring, or attaining the consciousness of the presence of God.

Seek the Substance

Whether it is the abundance of health or wealth, that abundance can come in no other way than by demonstrating the substance of which health and wealth are formed. A consciousness of God's presence always appears outwardly in the forms necessary for our immediate fulfillment. The command is to "seek ye first the kingdom of God, and his righteousness; and all these things shall be added unto you."[1] First of all, it is necessary to understand what the kingdom of God is and what is meant by that term. I learned that only through meditation could I gain that understanding, asking and seeking within the depths of my own being for the answer to that question. Out of that meditation came such explanations or synonyms as the realm of God, an awareness of God, or the consciousness of God. Through that, it dawned on me that the first thing I had to receive was a consciousness or an awareness of God. I had to penetrate through the appearance to the consciousness of God, and then, having achieved the awareness of God, all the things would be added.

It is much like saying that if we understood the principle of electricity we could have light, we could have heat, we could have cold, and we could have power. These would just be the various forms in which electricity could be made available to us. But without the principle of electricity, could we have electrical power? No, first must come the awareness of the principle of electricity and then would come the various forms of it.

God, the Substance of the Form

God is the substance of this universe. God made this world and all that is in the world. God made the crops in the ground. God made the ground even before the crops, the trees, the waters, the fish, and man. God made all this, but God is infinite, so out of what did God form this universe except out of the substance of Its own Self? It is God Itself that is the substance of everything we behold. Then how can we acquire anything separate and apart from that substance? How can we acquire anything without the awareness of the principle, substance, or life of which everything is formed?

This brings us to an important principle in our search for

the abundant life. First of all, we must give up all concern for the forms of good we are seeking. Those forms will come once we have the substance out of which they are made. And the substance of all is God. God is infinite divine consciousness, and it therefore becomes necessary to attain the consciousness of God, the conscious awareness of God, to come to a place in consciousness where we can say, "Yet in my flesh shall I see God,"[2] face to face. We come to the realization of God as the very presence, substance, law, and reality of our being. Having this consciousness, then, all forms of Consciousness appear.

We Entertain a Material Concept of a Spiritual Universe

One of the great mistakes that we make as human beings is to believe some things are separate and apart from spiritual substance. In other words, we have accepted the belief that there is a material creation. True, we believe that God can give us life, God can give us love, and God can give us truth, but when it comes to bread and butter and houses, we must go out and get these for ourselves because these are a universe apart from God. That is not true.

There is no selfhood apart from God, nor is there a creation apart from God. What we call a material creation is not a material creation: it is a *material sense* of the spiritual creation. When we come to the realization all creation is spiritual and there is not a material creation, but merely a *material sense* of a spiritual creation, everything in this universe answers, responds, and is subject to the divine consciousness which is God. If we had a whole row of twenty dollar gold pieces, they could not of themselves come to me or go from me to anyone else. They would stand right there forever. It would take some activity of consciousness to draw them to me or for them to be drawn to another person. If these twenty dollar gold pieces were material, they would not respond to consciousness. They are spiritual;

they are not material, but we entertain a material concept of them. It is so with everything in life.

God-Consciousness Individualized

We draw to ourselves our good through our own consciousness of truth and, if there were no other thing to prove it, the example of the gold pieces would in itself prove that all that exists, exists as forms of consciousness subject to the consciousness that formed them. When we begin with the realization that God is our consciousness and this consciousness is the substance, the law, and the activity unto all formation, we have stated the truth that makes us free from the belief of a separation from God and the things of God, the things of good.

This entire universe is embodied in our consciousness and is of our consciousness. Since God is our consciousness, then all things become subject to God, which really means subject to our individual consciousness of truth. To understand God as our individual consciousness is to understand the entire universe to be but forms and activities of our consciousness and subject to the divine consciousness, which is God but which is also our individual consciousness. Then we will never find ourselves separated from any form of good, for it is God's good pleasure to give us the kingdom. As a matter of fact we already have It; It is embodied within our consciousness.

Human Good or Spiritual Good?

One point that separates us from the demonstration of our good is our failure to understand the Master's statement, "Peace I leave with you, my peace I give unto you: not as the world giveth, give I unto you."[3] Even in dealing with the subject of supply, all of us on the spiritual path must ask ourselves these questions: Do we want the peace the world gives? Are we still determined to have our human will and human way fulfilled? Do we want our good to appear in the form that we believe to be for our good? Do we really mean it when we say we are seeking "My peace," that is, the Christ-peace?

We entertain a false or material sense of creation and we then want it to appear in the form of what we have decided constitutes our good. But on this very point we have the basic principle on which Christianity is founded and the difference between it and ancient Judaism, that is, the Judaism during the days of Jesus and his ministry of the Christ. The Hebrews were living out from a material state of consciousness, and their worship consisted in forms of ceremony, ritual, and creed. Their sense of good was entirely a human sense of good.

The Principle of Tithing

The Hebrews had high ideals of human good. They gave us the principle of tithing, of setting aside ten per cent of our possessions—land, cattle, whatever the form—for spiritual purposes. There is no higher human ideal than the setting aside of a portion of our possessions for an unselfish and impersonal good. Tithing became an evil only when the church adopted it as a means of income, emphasizing to their people that they must give up a certain amount for their soul's sake, thus imposing their will on them to show them that they needed protection and that the temple could give it to them, providing they tithed ten per cent of their income. The idea of tithing, as it was conceived by Abraham,[4] however, was a spiritual activity which, if followed today, would prove to be one of the greatest blessings in our individual as well as collective experience.

If we can perceive the benefit of expressing our gratitude for the furtherance of spiritual work, for the purpose of offering to others that which we through Spirit have discovered, or for benefits, some form of joy, or some service that we have already received, the ten per cent that we seem to have given away will come back to us as twenty, thirty, and fifty per cent. But if we let a single trace of belief enter our mind that in giving that ten per cent we are going to get something, we have rendered void the entire activity of tithing. It has then degenerated to an exchange or a deal with God, and it will not be successful.

Benefits of Tithing

There are outstanding experiences of men who in their desperation resorted to tithing. Considering themselves to be good men and faced with the imminent loss of all they possessed, they wondered why such losses had overtaken them, only to discover that they had left God out of their business and out of their lives, even though they probably went to church or to temple regularly.

One such person made an agreement with himself that if he ever got another job, no matter what it was, ten per cent of his earnings would go to some impersonal cause. When he finally secured a job, it was for only twenty dollars a week, but when he came home at the end of the first week with only eighteen dollars, his wife asked about the other two dollars. He reminded her of his promise to tithe, and her answer was, "Of course, that's a wonderful thing to do when we are on our feet, but how are we going to live and support a family on eighteen dollars a week? Twenty dollars is bad enough, but eighteen dollars is worse." Unperturbed, his response was, "How have we been supporting the family these weeks when I have been unemployed and had no income?" So, out of that twenty dollars, he gave two dollars as his spiritual gift. I knew this man later when he was giving eighty per cent of his income to charity and still had more than a hundred thousand dollars a year left for his family.

Another person who was driven to bankruptcy came to the conclusion that something must be wrong since he was a very religious man. The idea that he had left God out of his partnership came to him, and from that moment on he made the decision to take God into his business to the extent of ten per cent, not as a bribe but as a partner. He, too, found that eventually he was giving eighty per cent of his income to charity and yet had several hundred thousand dollars year after year for himself.

We are not human or mortal beings; we are not material beings: we are spiritual beings, children of God, "joint-heirs with Christ"[5] to all the heavenly riches. All that the Father has is ours. That is the actual truth of being, regardless of what the appearance to the contrary may be. How should we go about living that truth? By trying to get more or by sharing of the abundance that we already have? When we attempt to get something, to desire or want something, even something good, we are denying our divinity, our heirship with God. We are denying that we already are the children of God and that all that the Father has is ours.

Knowing Our True Identity, the Basis of Spiritual Living

There is only one way to live out from our true identity, and that is by, first of all, knowing what it is, secondly, accepting it, and thirdly, by living it. The only individual who is fulfilling a spiritual destiny is the one who is thinking of abundance as an act of giving, not an act of getting. No one can fulfill his destiny of the abundant life who has any thought of getting anything at any time from anybody. It is impossible to think of ourselves as spiritual beings and at the same time to desire something or to say we need something. There is only one thing we need, and that is to become more of an outlet for pouring out. It is as the Master said, "O Jerusalem, Jerusalem, thou that killest the prophets, and stonest them which are sent unto thee, how often would I have gathered thy children together, even as a hen gathereth her chickens under her wings, and ye would not!"[6] How he tried to point out to them that they must pour out, pour out, and pour out—let it flow, instead of sitting at his feet begging for more.

Tithing comes closer to the spiritual demonstration of supply than any other activity in human experience because tithing concerns itself with giving. It does not concern itself with getting. True tithing is the desire to give with no thought of a return.

Marriage: Failure or Success?

We can easily determine whether our love is spiritual or material by whether it concerns itself with giving and serving or with some benefit that we might receive. Harsh as it may sound, there is no real love that seeks a return, something for itself. That is why throughout the ages the institution of marriage has resulted in failure so many times. Those who marry often think only of some benefit they will derive from it. Even when two people agree that some mutual good will be derived, it is still not love. It is not love even if they both agree that one can bring one thing to a marriage and the other something else. That is not love; that is just a human bargain. The only type of love that is love is the love that wants to pour itself out with no thought of a return. It is that type of love in marriage that makes for the harmony, happiness, and permanence of marriage.

A couple, who were my friends for more than twenty years, had a marriage that lasted for fifty years. In all the years that I knew them, I never saw them together that they were not holding hands. Never was his voice raised above that of a conversational tone, and never once was it a question of "Will you get me this? Or will you give me this?" It was always a question on both sides, "Can I do this for you? Can I do that for you?" Never did one ask the other for anything—not in my hearing, and I was with them morning, noon, and night for many years because they were my closest friends. That one example, and probably an isolated example of love, is what I mean by attaining an awareness of abundance in the realization of our true identity, because in our true identity we have but one function and that is to serve. It does not make any difference whether it is husband or wife. It does not make any difference whether it is students, patients, friends, or business associates, we were placed here for only one purpose and that is to show forth the glory of God. And to whom would we show that forth except to one another?

How Truth Becomes Practical

If the transcendental spiritual truth were not practical, it would have no relationship with God and His creation. It is practical, but strange as it may seem in order to make it practical, we must begin with the understanding that we are not seeking the peace the world can give. We are not seeking the prosperity the world can give, the honors, and the glories of the world. We are seeking only that divine peace, which the Master called "My peace," the spiritual peace, the real peace. That can come only from a sense of service, sharing, and giving.

It changes our life completely and sometimes instantaneously when we learn to live for the purpose of letting the qualities and activities of God flow through, rather than always seeking to get something. When we understand that we have no righteousness of our own, no wealth of our own to give or bestow, that nothing exists that is a personal possession, then we are instruments for the Divine, instruments through which the one life flows, the one infinite abundance, the one wealth, all of God. "The earth is the Lord's, and the fulness thereof."[7] "Son, thou art ever with me, and all that I have is thine."[8]

"The earth is the Lord's, and the fulness thereof." There is nothing we have in our pocket that belongs to us. There is nothing that we have in the bank that belongs to us. It really gives one a good laugh to travel in an airplane, look down upon this big round earth, and see people and property with fences around them. How impossible it is to fence off God's universe and claim some part of it as our exclusive possession! It can't be mine and it can't be yours: it is God's. We are instruments for Its expression. We are vehicles, servants to the universe. We serve it as it serves us. There is no such thing as personal possessions in a spiritual universe.

Wealth Is a Trust

In looking out at life from a materialistic standpoint, it is true that the only answer to everything is to get: get, acquire, achieve. Those who have been successful at getting have discovered of what little value it is in bringing real happiness. The few exceptions have been those who have accepted their wealth as a trust, those who have had some measure of spiritual understanding along with their acquisitions and have understood that they hold them in trust for God.

On the whole the individual who brings forth the fullest measure of wealth or prosperity discovers that it does not result in an overabundance of material possessions. Instead it appears as infinite supply, infinite good, but not burdensome wealth, enabling a person to maintain his spiritual integrity and not become overwhelmed with possessions. Spiritual prosperity is a normal and natural experience for everyone, just as health and immortality are.

Only Spiritual Wholeness and Spiritual Prosperity Are Permanent

If we try to acquire health through material means and if we had a whole retinue of physicians and surgeons with all that is included in expert medical care, these medical practitioners could keep us in health only up to a certain point and for a certain number of years. After that, in spite of their very best efforts, health would degenerate into disease and ultimately death. On the other hand, spiritually discerned, health is a permanent dispensation and never dependent on outer conditions. Health, harmony, wholeness, completeness, and immortality are all ours and are not subject to outer conditions once we attain them through spiritual realization and maintain that awareness.

In the material universe, life is dependent on the actions of the heart, liver, and lungs, that is, the organs and functions of the body. In spiritual understanding, the organs and functions of the body are dependent upon the life which we are. We are the life; we are the soul and the substance of our being. That life which we are acts in and through our body and maintains it and sustains it unto eternity. There never would or should be such a thing as a sign of age after we gain the realization that it is not the body that acts upon life, but life that acts upon the body.

Material sense tells us that our life is dependent on the action of the body. Spiritual sense reverses that and says that the action of our body is dependent upon our soul, our consciousness, our life, the Spirit. It is the spirit of God dwelling in us that governs our body. Material sense tells us that wealth is dependent on how much money we have, but spiritual sense reverses that and says that our consciousness of God determines how much money we will have.

A Material Sense
of a Spiritual Universe

This is a spiritual universe about which we are entertaining a material sense. Once we reverse that material sense and are established in spiritual awareness, we discover the truth of being that sets us free. Free from what? From material sense—not from sin, disease, and death, but from the material sense of life and wholeness. In reality there is no such thing as sin, disease, and death. In reality, if any man has ever died in the history of the world, the whole principle of God is invalidated because God is life eternal and God is infinite. So there could not be any life that could ever pass into death. There could not be one trace of consciousness ever becoming unconscious. If there were, then the whole principle of God disappears off the face of the earth. Certainly, material sense will testify to death.

Material sense will say that wealth is dependent on numbers of dollars and health is dependent on the harmonious functioning of the organs of the body. If we continue entertaining a material sense of health and wealth, it will not be too long before the organs and functions of the body are not operating properly and, therefore, life is fading or the dollars are disappearing and with them the prosperity.

The Miracles of the Bible

Spiritual teachers or practitioners do not give us dollar bills or healthy organs and functions. Instead, they help students come into the spiritual awareness of the Master's statement, "Peace I leave with you, my peace I give unto you: not as the world giveth, give I unto you." They give us the realization of our true identity. Know you not that "ye are gods"? "The Spirit itself beareth witness with our spirit, that we are children of God: And if children, then heirs; heirs of God, and joint-heirs with Christ."[10] *My* peace, the Christ-peace, reveals to us our true identity: I am not body, I am life eternal.

When we see that point, we begin to understand the so-called miracles of the Bible. As long as there was a Moses, there was manna, water flowing from the rocks, and clothing that waxed not old. As long as there was a Jesus, the multitudes were fed and healed. To him, matter could have no effect on man's true identity. When Jesus turned from the appearance of death, life appeared. Because he was a miracle worker? No, he said it was his Father and our Father that did this, not just a special gift given to him.

The entire ministry of Jesus proved that since "I am the way, the truth, and the life,"[11] *I* is the principle of existence, the substance of supply, the substance of health, the substance and activity of life. *I* am that. To ourselves, gently and quietly, let us say *I:*

> *I, I, I. I* am the substance of life.
> *I,* that *I* at the center of my being,
> is the law and the continuity of life.
> It is the activity of life animating,
> governing, and feeding the body.
> *I* am the meat. *I* am the wine. *I* am the water.

> It is not the food I eat that is the strength
> of my body: it is the *I* of me which is the meat,
> the wine, and the water unto my body,
> the all-sustaining food.
> The food I eat does not sustain me:
> *I* am the food that sustains me.
> *I,* the principle within, feeds, supports, strengthens,
> and maintains my body and my supply,
> even to producing gold from the fish's mouth
> and multiplying loaves and fishes.
> That same principle of *I* becomes the law of harmony
> and multiplication unto my supply.

Health and wealth both flow from the within to the without. If we are sitting, waiting for these to come to us, we have acknowledged our separation from them and accepted the inevitability of disease and lack. That must be the inescapable outcome, if we sit waiting, expecting good to come to us.

Good Is Our Experience in Proportion to Our Pouring Forth

Miracles happen once we give up the materialistic belief that we need something more added to us than what we already have. It is much as if we were to say, "I need integrity." We cannot need integrity. We already have it, but many of us are not utilizing it. Everyone has integrity. The thief on the cross had integrity, or Jesus could not have taken him into heaven with him in that one day. He had not reformed or joined a church or truth-movement, yet he was taken into heaven that very day, because he had all the necessary integrity, but up to that moment he had not drawn on it.

So it is with us. We have all the necessary prosperity, health, and wealth. The problem is that we are not letting them flow out from us. We are sitting here as if we really were material, limited, finite beings, waiting for some good to come to us. The streetcar never passes that corner. We can wait forever for good to come to us and it will never come.

We can begin as the poor widow did with her mite, but pour we must; and we must begin to pour out whatever mite we have, share it, give it, release it, thereby demonstrating that our faith is not in it. The widow sharing with Elijah gave all she had, that handful of meal and a bit of oil, and then she found that there was no end to the supply. It multiplied itself. Giving or sharing is a principle of life, a spiritual principle. This is not said in the sense of asking any person to tithe, but in the sense of urging everyone to acknowledge the infinite nature of his own being.

The purpose of the message of the Infinite Way is to reveal the infinite nature of individual being, your being, my being, and every person's being. How can students accept the writings of the Infinite Way as to the infinite nature of individual being and then try to demonstrate supply? It will not and cannot work. The only way in which we can demonstrate supply is to begin with whatever it is we have, whether it is money, service, patience, cooperation, or gratitude. Whatever it is, begin with something, and begin to pour it. Begin to get it out. Above everything, resist the temptation to accept the belief that there is a selfhood, your selfhood or my selfhood, that needs something, requires something, must have something.

If we are following the teaching of the Master, Christ Jesus, we must accept the truth that in order to find our life, we must lose it. There is no better way for us to find spiritual immortality and spiritual prosperity than to give up that personal sense of selfhood that says, "I need; I require; I want; I should have; I deserve." That personal sense of "I" is our devil, and it must be given up.

We Let the Christ of
Our Being Fulfill Every Demand

God is an infinite reservoir of strength and wisdom. Consciously connected with that reservoir, no matter how much work we did we would not be weary or tired unless we were indulging in a selfhood apart from God. That is the life that must be given up: the life that can be weary, the life that can be tired, the life that can be overworked, the life of which too much is demanded. The only life is God, and there can be no demand made upon It that is too much. If any demand is made upon us, it is not really made upon us: it is made upon the Christ of our being. So we step aside with the attitude, "All right, I have no objection to fulfilling this demand if the Christ of me will do it." Then every demand made upon us will be fulfilled whether it is for a thousand healings or for a thousand dollars.

Whatever demand is legitimately made upon us is not made upon us: it is made upon the Christ of us. If some demand is made upon us that is illegitimate, we should take the same attitude, because if it is really an illegitimate demand, it will never have to be met. The Christ will find a way to dissolve even that demand. That is important. We never have to be afraid of an injustice once we have taken our stand as spiritual beings. If some persons seem to demand more of us than they have a right to demand, we realize that if the Christ of us can supply it, we

are perfectly willing. If it is not a legitimate demand, the Christ
will dissolve that demand made upon us. Otherwise It will meet
it, once we have removed that personal sense of "I" that is self-
righteous, has a need, or a requirement.

I Have

Since we have entertained a material sense of existence and
have to reverse ourselves to get back to the spiritual sense, it is
helpful to remember the statement of the Master: "Peace I leave
with you, my peace I give unto you: not as the world giveth,
give I unto you." In other words, we keep before ourselves the
idea that we are not seeking material good in any form but only
spiritual good and that we have meat to eat that the world
knows not of.

Whatever the demand made upon us, whether it is for bodily strength, mental strength, moral strength, or whether it is a
demand made upon us financially, we remember that we have
meat the world knows not. The world may judge how much we
have of health, wealth, strength, harmony, or length of years.
Our view must be not to judge by appearances but to answer to
the world's judgment:

> I have meat that the world knows not of.
> I have an inner substance, an inner supply,
> an inner bank account, sufficient to meet every
> demand that is made upon me from the outer.

Once we acknowledge that we have an inner meat, an inner
wine, an inner water, a spiritual substance that the world cannot
see, touch, hear, taste, or smell, from that moment we have
demonstrated spiritual abundance, and it will appear in the
outer realm as everything necessary for our unfoldment. But the
beginning of it is to make the acknowledgment:

I have meat the world knows not of.
If you were to ask me for water,
I could give it to you. I can give you loaves
and fishes. I can give you words of truth
without number, unto infinity.
Ask of me, and I will give you life eternal, because
I have the substance of life eternal within me.

I have the word of God and the word of God
is meat, drink, and clothing.
The word of God is health and wealth.
The word of God is life eternal, and I have that.
I have an infinite wellspring of water. I have the wine
of inspiration in the *I* that I am, and that *I* is the
spiritual substance within my own being.

As long as we can realize we have that spiritual substance, we will not withhold anything that may be required: hours of service, hours of meditation, hours of speaking, or even dollar bills. It does not make any difference what it is. Any legitimate demand brings that inward recognition: "Come unto me, all ye that labor and are heavy laden, and I will give you rest."[12] Out of what? Out of the word of God, out of the inner meat that the world knows not of, out of this wellspring of water that is within us.

As we realize that truth, we will be "dying daily" to our humanhood and will be reborn of the Spirit. We will no longer be born of flesh, but of the Spirit. Then we can pour it out from now until doomsday and still have it all left over to share.

Prosperity or abundance comes out of the substance of love, and love is God. It is not your love; it is not my love. It is the love of God. Instead of trying to love, instead of trying to be more loving, we let God flow through us; let God express Its love through us.

Chapter Seven

Freedom Through Grace

Instead of looking outside to the world of men and things for our good, we must develop the ability to turn to the kingdom of God within our own being and let our good flow from that kingdom within, rather than expecting our good to come from persons or things. But even if we accept the truth that the kingdom of God is within us, that our soul is the storehouse of our good, and that within us is the activity, law, and substance of our good, how do we bring it forth into manifestation or expression? How do we come into the awareness of it? How do we come into the realization of this good appearing in our outer world?

In the spiritual world, that is, the spiritual kingdom, everything unfolds through the power of grace. The first requirement in living by grace is to understand that this is a spiritual universe and that our good is spiritual, all stored up within our own being, within our very consciousness. Instead of looking outside, we learn to look within, and this very act of turning from the outside world to the within starts the flow of the power of grace into expression for us. We have nothing to do with bringing forth the power of grace except the withdrawal of our attention from the outer world.

All Good Was Established
Within Our Consciousness in the Beginning

When we agree within ourselves that we will not speak about any apparent need of "man, whose breath is in his nostrils,"[1] or look outside ourselves for fulfillment, but that from now on we are going to turn to the kingdom within, the power of grace takes over. Grace cannot come into expression while we are looking to the outer realm, because when we look outside, it is as if we had shut off that particular source of supply, and there is no way for it to flow. Where we reverse that, however, and turn our attention from what we know out here to the within, it is as if something took the cap off, and the flow from within begins.

All good—every form of life, every form of love, every form of truth, every form of substance, every activity and every law—is within our own being and was established there since "before Abraham." At the very moment of our co-existence with God, all that the Father has was established within our own being, everything: integrity, loyalty, fidelity, cooperativeness, joy, peace, harmony, gratitude, every conceivable thing. It includes all those things that constitute home, that constitute transportation, protection, safety, security, and freedom. All of those qualities and activities are established within our own being.

We have made the mistake of going outside and expecting them from a government, from an army, or from an investment. Always we have looked to something external, but now we are told to get back within. The very instant of our turning within starts the activity of divine grace. It may seem to begin in a small way, in an insignificant way at first, as if the cap that was fastened over our pipeline were being removed slowly, letting our good trickle forth. But it is only a short time before that cap is completely removed, and the activity of grace takes over.

Humility, Requisite
to the Flow of Grace

The activity of grace comes into its fullness in proportion as we learn to drop the word, "I." The word "I," that is,
the personal sense of "I," is the devil that gets in the way of
divine grace. The moment I say that I must do this, do that,
or wonder what I should do about this, what steps I should
take, or how I should go about this, I dam up the flow of
divine grace.

When we rest and relax in the sense of "I can of mine own
self do nothing,"[2] thereby giving up one's self, the power of
divine grace takes over, and It never stops flowing unless we let
that personal sense of "I" take over again. We stop the flow once
we begin to think "I of my own self have done this," or "I with
my understanding have accomplished it," or "I with my superi-
or wisdom or power have done this."

Divine grace takes over in proportion to our humility, and
our humility is that state of mind we reach when we realize
that even if we would we cannot. Even if we would like to
heal, you and I cannot do that. As much as we might humanly love to give all our friends and relatives a complete, perfect,
and instantaneous healing, we cannot do it. But the Father
within us can.

In that moment of relaxation from personal effort, a relaxation from the belief of personal powers, which I call *humility*,
divine grace takes over and proves what It can do, and It does it
often in most remarkable ways. It does it without our personally knowing who is blessed or at what moment or in what way it
happens. It is so completely free of all personal sense that we can
have the experience I have had when people came to me to tell
me that some particular experience happened at a certain time.
I am grateful that I knew nothing about it at the time. It was the
free flowing of the divine power of God, and there was nothing
human about it. It was the Spirit Itself that went forth.

Only God Can Do

As we overcome the belief that we can do this, that we would like to do such and such a thing, or that with our understanding we should be able to work some "miracle," we let go and realize that the more understanding we think we have, the less we will be able to do. If we can accept the truth that the more understanding we believe we have, the less we will be able to do, then we will realize what it means to let divine grace take over and discover that real understanding consists of the knowledge that "I can of mine own self do nothing." That is the understanding, the true understanding, the spiritually humble understanding, which opens the way for the power within to take over.

It was ordained right from the beginning that we should let God live our life. It was ordained from the beginning that God is forever expressing Itself as our individual being, maintaining and sustaining the universe in Its own image and likeness to show forth Its handiwork. We are that perfect work; but only in proportion as we let that power operate through us does It show Itself forth as the harmony and perfection of our existence.

Prayer

Once we realize that we have nothing of ourselves to give, nothing of ourselves to do or to know, but that even the knowing and the praying are really activities of the Father within, then we will come to this point toward which we have been working, and that is to the realization of the true nature of prayer. We might ultimately come to a concept or understanding of prayer in which we would find our prayers answered.

It is through prayer that we must make our contact with God, and it is through the right understanding of prayer that the activity, the grace, the love, and the life of God are made manifest in our experience. This brings us to that particular phase or understanding of prayer which is called grace. We ourselves cannot bring forth the activity of grace, since grace is the gift and the activity of God.

Self-Effacement

Grace is something that expresses in us or through us. Grace is something that comes to us without our deserving It, without our being worthy of It. Grace is what happened to the thief on the cross, who certainly from no human standpoint was deserving of being taken into heaven that day. Yet the Master promised to do just that, showing that divine grace had not only wiped out the sins of the thief, but also all the punishment due for these sins.

What was it that enabled that thief in just a short while to prepare himself for the experience of heaven, for the action of grace and forgiveness in his life? Humility. In his final moment of distress, he must have realized, "Why, I am nothing. I should have let this divine power flow through me, and none of the evil deeds would have been necessary." The thief on the cross must have recognized what a failure he had been. There is nothing more productive of progress in the spiritual universe than to acknowledge Jesus' statement, "I can of mine own self do nothing."[2] "If I bear witness of myself, my witness is not true."[3] Such an admission of his own inability to do might seem like failure, but he recognized there was that within him that could do all things: "The Father that dwelleth in me, he doeth the works."[4]

We make way for that divine power to come forth in proportion to our acknowledgment that we can do nothing, know nothing, heal nothing, supply nothing, be nothing, even be failures, but that we live, not of ourselves but the Christ lives our life. "I and my Father are one,"[5] but the Father is greater than I. "Greater is he that is in you, than he that is in the world."[6] There has to be a relaxation, a kind of getting in back of ourselves in order to let this He that is within us come forth into manifestation and expression. It is as if we were to say, "Come forth," and then let It flow out. It is in that act of stepping back or stepping aside, as if to let It flow out or come forward, that divine grace takes over.

The Meaning of Idolatry

The beginning of wisdom is to recognize that man cannot do for us. Money in the bank, investments, and business are but avenues, vehicles, or channels, but are not the source of supply. When that is recognized and realized, divine grace takes over but only in the moment that we release our faith or dependence on the external. Many persons who have striven for healing through metaphysical or spiritual help without receiving it have one day realized that they were relying on external help and decided that there is just no use of relying on anything out there. In that instant they were healed.

When we remove our reliance on anything external, something within picks us up. The law involved in giving up an outer reliance and dependence goes back to the commandment about idolatry: "Thou shalt not make unto thee any graven image. . . . Thou shalt not bow down thyself to them, nor serve them."[7] Idolatry is the faith, hope, or confidence that we have in anything out here.

Food and Spirituality

Eating meat or not eating meat could be an example of idolatry. If humanly I should ask you to give up eating meat and you agreed to do this, your faith in the nutriments that are supposed to be in meat would not have been removed, so I would have to give you a substitute for meat. As long as you had a substitute for meat, such as enough eggs, cheese, or nuts, you would have the equivalent for the meat, and you would do just as well physically as if you were eating meat. There is nothing spiritual about giving up meat and substituting something else for it because your reliance is still on something in the outer realm, so what difference does it make on what you are depending? It is not what goes into the mouth that defiles. It is what comes out, and what has come out is that your faith was not in God or Spirit but in that substance we call meat.

If you had a spiritual healing in which the desire for meat dropped away from you, however, you would not have to look around for a substitute food because the Spirit would have taken over, and the Spirit then becomes your food. You would have demonstrated that you do not live by bread or meat alone but by every word of God. You would not need to think about providing a substitute if through spiritual development you had lost your taste for it. Whatever meat supplied would now be taken care of by the Spirit, and you would be led to eat whatever would be necessary. That is as clear an explanation as I can give of the idea of not depending on anything in the outer realm but permitting the Spirit to take over.

Withdraw Faith from and
Reliance on the Forms of Supply

I do not ask you to give away all your money because in reality you do not need it. As long as there remains a certain degree of faith in your mind in that x amount of money that is stored away in the vault, the possession of that money gives a certain feeling of security. If you give it away because you are told to do so, you are likely to get hurt because you have nothing to take the place of that in which you had placed your faith. But if through spiritual unfoldment you come to the realization that the kingdom of God is within you, that *I* within you am the source of that which is out there, you could give your money away, and the next day find yourself with literally twice as much, because instead of a very limited amount of money you would have an infinite amount of Spirit pouring through.

The whole subject of idolatry is bound up in the degree of faith or confidence you have in the things or persons in the outer realm. For example, every woman must come to a place in consciousness where she realizes that her supply not only is not dependent on her husband, father, or child, but where she actually has demonstrated her own source of supply separate and apart from any member of her family.

I have always cautioned wives, however, not to tell their husbands that they do not need his check anymore. They should wait a while for that awareness to become realized consciousness. But they must begin to understand that even though now that is an avenue or vehicle of supply for them, it is not their source of supply. Their dependence is not on it and, if it were cut off, instantly the Spirit would produce another form of supply, and through that they would work up gradually to that state of consciousness in which they would understand God to be the source of their supply. Then a husband could keep his whole check without any loss to the wife because her income would flow in through another avenue, but always from the one source.

There is no limitation that would make it impossible for a person's own income to come to him. There is no limit to the activity of Spirit. If through spiritual unfoldment a person were able to remove her faith in her husband's or father's income or in her investments, she would soon discover that Spirit would provide for her much more abundantly and generously than she had ever know in the past.

This is true of men as well as women. A man may have a job or a business and, at the moment, that is his avenue of supply. But he must not accept that as the source of his income but merely as the avenue or vehicle for it at the present time.

If you have transferred your allegiance from the outer to the Infinite Invisible within, and the day should come when there is no business, no trade, or no investments on which to rely, you would find, as Moses did, that manna would fall from the sky and water come from the rocks. There is a source of supply entirely separate and apart from your human activity, and it is even more abundant and brought forth with less labor than is our usual daily activity. It is not that you retire or give up your jobs and say, "Now, God, You take care of me," for there is no such God. God is your individual consciousness, a consciousness of omnipresence, omnipotence, and omniscience. As you develop your awareness of that spirit of God in you, It takes over through the power of grace and finds ways for supply to come to you.

Spiritual Healing and Medicine

The truth that consciousness is the source of all good is true also in the area of health problems. When people come to me who have no background of truth, who are in the hospital under *materia medica,* who have been depending on digitalis or some other form of medication without which they are sure they would die, they may ask, "Must I give that up immediately?" To cut them off from some such remedy while still retaining their full faith and dependence on it might be a very difficult, if not impossible, thing for them to do. My usual answer is, "No, I am not going to say to you to cut that off right now if you do not think you can make that demonstration. But I am asking you to lose your faith in it because something greater than it must come through."

For a short time then I stand by with everything I have and know in order to give them the opportunity to experience their freedom. But if I see that they are so completely bound to their faith in the external that they cannot make a change, then I explain to them that there is no use trying to ride two horses in the same race forever. It cannot be done. You have to choose this day whom you will serve: God or mammon.

It is not a question as to whether God has any prejudice against medicine. That is not the point. The point is that when you place your faith in the outer, you do not give the inner a chance to operate. It is only when you drop your faith in the things outside that this cap uncovers itself and comes forth. You have to do that. "Choose you this day whom ye will serve."[8] While your attention is out here, you are not listening to the flow from within you and it is dammed up. When you withdraw your attention from the outer and no longer place your faith in that dead stuff out there because of the assurance that you have the creative principle of all life within you, the presence within takes over, and It works in miraculous ways.

How Great Is Our Faith?

Many years ago when Mark Twain sailed to Europe, he was taken quite ill on the steamer. As he got off the ship at the end of the journey, reporters met him and said, "Oh, Mr. Twain, we have many cables here from your friends in America asking us to tell you that they were praying for you from the moment they heard you were sick." His response was, "I hope you will cable back and tell them that I am sure their prayers did me no harm."

You can be equally certain that most of those prayers did him no good. That type of prayer has little value because there is no principle behind it. How can you pray God to heal you and at the same time feel that you must have some external form as an adjunct to God? "Oh ye of little faith."[9] "If ye have faith as a grain of mustard seed, ye shall say unto this mountain, Remove hence to yonder place; and it shall remove; and nothing shall be impossible unto you."[10] It is not that everything on earth is not our interpretation of some part of God's creation. That has nothing to do with it. It has to do with a state of consciousness.

Is it not strange that although we have taken the Master as our example and our way shower, we disbelieve almost everything he told us? When it came to healing his question was, "Believe ye that I am able to do this?"[11] And when the disciples could not heal and asked Jesus why they had failed he said, "Because of your unbelief."[10] It is not that everything on earth is not our interpretation of some part of God's creation, that has nothing to do with it. It has to do with a state of consciousness. Again we are told that in Jerusalem "he did not many mighty works there because of their unbelief."[12]

By their works, truth-teachings should show forth the activity of the Christ. When we begin to show forth what a truth-teaching will do for us, we bring one, two, twelve, twenty, thirty, fifty right along with us into the work because the world is hungry for harmony. The world is hungry for health, for protection, for safety. People are turning more to spiritual literature because they have found that mere right thinking is not the answer: God is the answer. But in how many truth-movements is God the central theme, the only power? We succeed in showing that forth to the world when we lose our belief or faith in the outer realm and look not to bread, but to the spirit of God to feed, sustain, and uphold us. Even if the first break is difficult for a day, a week, or a month, we must stand fast. Beginners can be excused if it takes a little longer for them.

Choose This Day

Those persons who for years have looked to a spiritual teaching for help and have wondered why they have not received it to the degree they expected it are trying to swim across the lake and at the same time hold fast to the shore. We have to be willing to start out and sink or swim. Of course it really does not make any difference whether we sink or swim because, as long as our faith is in God, we are perfectly all right. "Yea, though I walk through the valley of the shadow of death, I will fear no evil,"[13] for God goes with me. What difference whether we sink or swim? If we sink the waters cannot drown us. If we walk through the fire[14] the flames cannot kindle upon us. *I Am* is in the midst of us, and our faith is in that *I* at the center of our being, in that divine consciousness. It is up to us.

We have to choose sooner or later, and it might as well be sooner. We all have to come to that point where we are willing for divine grace to take over. But divine grace will not take over while we are holding to something on the outer plane, nor will It take over as long as our dependence is on person or thing, rather than on the activity of truth in our consciousness. Many persons who have realized the presence and power of God came to that realization by grace Itself, not even knowing how it happened or why. Most of us are not in that category and so if we are to come to grace we will come through knowing how and why.

In the books the mystics wrote or that were written about them, we cannot see how they came to that place of divine grace where the spirit of God took over. I can tell you that it is done in that second when we withdraw our faith and confidence from the person, thing, or circumstance outside and recognize that from now on the kingdom of God, the Christ within us, is our support. We will know that, once we really experience the flow of the Christ in our whole heart, soul, mind, and body, the feeling of that substance or essence that we may never have dreamed was already established within us, waiting to flow forth, but kept dammed up because we were holding on to something out here and thereby keeping this Christ squeezed in.

Do We Trust the Word of God?

Our reliance on person, place, or thing is the blocking point that might prevent us from attaining the thing we are trying to achieve. God does not get in our way. The Christ does not play favorites. There are no powers outside of us that can prevent our demonstration. The only thing in the world that can prevent our demonstration is what takes place within us. It is not what enters from without but what goes out from within, that is, in what state of consciousness we find ourselves. If we are in that state where we cannot let go, nothing can be done about it. But if we are close to the point of realization, consciously we take the step of admitting to ourselves that there is a presence and power within us greater than any opposition outside, greater than any circumstance or condition, greater than any sin or disease.

Let us make that acknowledgment and hold fast to it for the next few days, trying to come to a state of mind where we are able to trust the word of God more than anything in the external world, reaching that point of confidence in which we can realize that if the same Spirit "that raised up Jesus from the dead dwell in [us], he that raised up Christ from the dead shall also quicken [our] mortal bodies by his Spirit that dwelleth in [us],"[15] if so be the confidence and faith in the power and presence of God dwell in us. It can do as much for us and our body as it did for Jesus and his body or Jairus' daughter and her body, or Lazarus and his body.

Peter tells us that the same Spirit, the same God of Abraham, Isaac, and Jacob raised up the man at the Temple Gate Beautiful. There is no different God today. It is the same God of Abraham, Isaac, and Jacob. Before them it was the same God of Krishna and Buddha. Now it happens to be our God. It is the same God, the same principle, the same law. The only difference is that somebody in those days had enough faith to stop relying on material means and trust the kingdom of God within his own being.

Now we come to that place of recognition. Do you believe that this was the word of God? Do you believe that this was true? Do you believe that this was the Word as it is given to us in scripture? Do you believe that this is the very message that our Master was giving on the shore of Galilee? Do you believe that he was saying at that time the same truth you are reading here that you have water within your own being that is greater than all the water that is in Jacob's well?

When Jesus was in the wilderness, tempted, and said, "Get thee behind me, Satan,"[16] implying that he did not need an external demonstration, do you believe that he was telling you the same thing that you are reading in this letter? This letter is merely bringing back to your attention the same message, the same mission, the same truth that Jesus gave to his people, repeating to you again the admonition to have faith as a grain of mustard seed, not faith in pills, powders, vitamins, and food, not faith in banks, trust companies, and bonds. But unless you have faith that the kingdom of God is within you, unless you have an understanding faith that God has given Itself to you— "Son, . . . all that I have is thine"[17]—unless you can realize that, the whole message and mission of Christianity is lost again.

They That Take Up the Sword

It is later than you think. It is later than you think because the whole world stands on the brink of a volcano, placing its last bit of faith for survival in a bomb, in an atom, in something that is less than an atom: a broken up atom. That is a poor crutch upon which to lean. The Master instructed, "All they that take up the sword shall perish with the sword."[18] If you could wipe out every enemy that exists on earth today with atomic or hydrogen bombs, under the law of the Master you would have just sealed your own doom. When the bomb fell on Hiroshima, the Third World War began for us, and the loss of thousands of men. Why? Why are we likely to lose thousands of men? We lived by dropping an atomic bomb over Japan, and we may die because the same bomb is now held by the so-called enemy.

Why do we not believe the Master? Why do we not understand when he tells us that if we live by the sword we will die by the sword? Let us understand that if we live by outer things, we will die by outer things. In the end we have to learn to live by the word of God, to abide in God, and let God abide in us, and let the word of God abide in us. This word of truth—not words in a book but in consciousness—this Word in our consciousness is food, medicine, the strength of our bones, the blood, the flesh, the substance of life, the activity of life. Some day the world has to believe the Master, and this is as good a day as any other.

There is a story that comes down to us from the ancient Orientals of a married couple who, through some inner conversion, had come to the spiritual path and the realization that life meant fulfillment from within. Because both of them had realized it at the same time they gave away their possessions and decided to go up and down the highways and byways and live from within through grace. They felt they did not need any particular home site; they were just traveling, walking wherever they wanted to walk, and enjoying themselves as they went, living by an inner grace.

One day the husband was walking a few feet in front of his wife when he bent over, picked up something, looked at it, rubbed it on his robe, looked at it again, and put it in his pocket. His wife came up and tapped him on the shoulder and asked, "What was that you picked up?" "Why," he answered, "it was a diamond." "Oh," she said, "I noticed that you rubbed the dust off it and threw that away. Was the diamond any more valuable than the dust?" That is our lesson. Is one thing in the outer realm more valuable to us than another, or is all the value in the divine grace within our own being?

Trust in the Lord

There are certain Bible passages which, when realized in consciousness, become the substance, activity, and law of our daily experience. Let me share some that have helped students to make the transition from the ups and downs of human existence to the straight and narrow path of spiritual existence.

> Trust in the Lord with all thine heart; and lean not
> unto thine own understanding. In all thy ways
> acknowledge him, and he shall direct thy paths.
>
> Proverbs: 3:5,6

Let us divide this passage and give each part special study. "Trust in the Lord with all thine heart." Here we bring to ourselves the full meaning of trusting the Infinite Invisible with a complete surrender of fear or doubt. "Lean not unto thine own understanding" is a renunciation of our self—personal powers, personal strength or wisdom, even personal goodness—in the knowledge that God, the consciousness of us, is the infinite intelligence and law unto our affairs.

"In all thy ways acknowledge him," thereby acknowledging that God is the source of our supply; God is the bond that links us with our fellow man, with animals and minerals. God is the activity of our body and business. God is the attraction in all human relationships. God is the only government. We could continue such a contemplation, including every avenue of our existence until the realization comes that God is directing our every path for us.

The Word in Our Consciousness Is All Things to Us

And Jesus answered him, saying,
It is written, That man shall not live by bread alone,
but by every word of God.

Luke 4:4

Here is another foundation stone in the message of the Infinite Way to be contemplated and meditated upon over and over until it becomes the very fabric of our being. We must remember, declare, and realize that we do not live alone by effects, such as food, vitamins, minerals, money, or investments, nor are we protected alone by bomb shelters, blackouts, mountain caves, or armaments. Rather our lives, our safety, and our security are dependent upon our consciousness of truth. The word of God in our consciousness is the bread of life, the safety and the security of our life. Our dependence is never on effect in any form, not even on the book called the Bible encased in steel plates, but in every word of God.

In Quietness and in Confidence

Awake, students of the Infinite Way. I am trying with every breath in me to turn your thoughts away from the peace of this world to the Christ-peace, *My* peace, the spiritual embodiment of heavenly good. Come now and take this step with me out of worldly peace into the spiritual kingdom.

> In quietness and in confidence shall be your strength.
> Isaiah 30:15

Seek not for strength or health in statements or in declarations, but in quietness and in confidence. In times of pain, sorrow, or discord, sit down or lie down and, instead of letting the mind race around with metaphysical thoughts, rest and relax. Say to the mind, "Peace, be still," and just rest back on that spiritual pillow in quietness and in confidence. Finally, rest in these inspiring passages from Luke and Matthew:

> Take no thought for your life,
> what ye shall eat; neither for the body,
> what ye shall put on. . . . Your Father knoweth that
> ye have need of these things. . . for it is your Father's
> good pleasure to give you the kingdom.
> Luke 12:22,30,32

> Seek ye first the kingdom of God,
> and his righteousness; and all these things
> shall be added unto you.
> Matthew 6:33

Chapter Eight

The Spiritual Life

As long as we live out from material sense, there will be discord, inharmony, ills, and evils. Only as we are able to make the transition to the spiritual consciousness of existence can we live free of the ups and downs, the good and evil, the health and sickness of material sense.

God cannot be brought to the material sense of life. Mortal or material man cannot please God. "So then they that are in the flesh cannot please God. But ye are not in the flesh, but in the Spirit, if so be that the spirit of God dwell in you. Now if any man have not the spirit of Christ, he is not his. . . . For as many as are led by the spirit of God, they are the sons of God."[1] Continuing as mortal and material man, attempting to live the life that we were born into and brought up in and, at the same time, expecting to bring spiritual good or the activity of the Christ into our life must result in failure. No, first there must be a transition from the material sense of existence to the spiritual consciousness of life.

What Characterizes Spiritual Existence?

What is the major difference between the material sense of existence and the spiritual? In a material sense of existence, the necessary and essential things of life are found in the external: in dollars, investments, physical conditions of good, business, companionship, and home. These are all considered vital, and so all material existence is aimed at attaining more companionship, more happiness, more homes, more or better transportation, more of this or more of that, always centered on the external.

Living out from the spiritual sense of existence, we recognize that we do not live by bread alone but by every word of God. Through that, we gain the understanding that the real meat of life is not the meat in a butcher shop but the meat the world knows not, and that is the spiritual substance of existence.

We begin to understand the mystical or transcendental terms the Master used. "If thou knewest the gift of God, and who it is that saith to thee, Give me to drink; thou wouldest have asked of him, and he would have given thee living water. . . . The water that I shall give him shall be in him a well of water springing up into everlasting life."[2] There was water in the well, but Jesus was not speaking of that; he did not have even a bucket with which to draw it. But he knew that he had a water that was far more important than the water in the well because anyone who drank of his water would not thirst again. In referring to the bread, the wine, and the water, he was continuously bringing to light the realization that there is something within our being that really is the substance, the law, and the activity of harmonious existence.

Learning to Rely on the Inner Substance

In order to bring the realization of this divine substance within us into full expression, at least for a while, we must devote ourselves to practice. To illustrate, let us suppose that I am a salesman and I have buyers with whom to deal. According to the human picture, the buyers decide whether or not they will buy from me and how much they will buy. Furthermore, the more I can sell them or the more I can compel them to buy from me, the better salesman I will be. Divine intelligence and Its activity, however, may dictate that some persons who are buying from me should not be buying, or they are buying more than they should, or they should stop buying entirely. That would be the act of an infinite divine principle that we call love.

On the other hand, those who are not buying all my products or not buying enough of them to satisfy the demands of the intelligence governing their own business, through divine intelligence would begin to act more intelligently in regard to their business, and that would perhaps mean buying more of my products.

Operating from the spiritual principle that I have no life and no mind of my own, but the life and mind of me is God, then I understand that not only is the life and mind of the salesman God, but the life and mind of the buyer is God and therefore, it no longer lies within the prerogative of the buyer to determine whether or not he will buy from me and how much. Then instead of a salesman going to a customer and wondering if he is going to buy, what mood he is going to be in today, or whether somebody else has gotten there ahead of him, the salesman's attitude would be: There is only one mind and that is the only mind that is functioning or can function, so I am going to the buyer knowing full well that the mind of God will speak through that buyer.

Insurance today is sold not merely to cover the needs of a family after the death of the wage earner, but insurance covers a much wider field of human use today. There are many persons who have a natural dislike for buying insurance as if it were taking money out of their pocket for something intangible, money they could use for something more tangible. That is not always an intelligent approach to the subject of insurance. If the insurance salesman can realize that he is not selling a material product, but the human symbol of divine protection, the human symbol of intelligent wisdom, and that it is the mind of God that controls its activity and its sale, he has lifted the selling of insurance above the decision of the prospect, above the head of "man, whose breath is in his nostrils,"³ and has realized that man cannot determine for himself whether or not he should have insurance or how much, but that the divine intelligence of that man would be the determining factor. If insurance were the nearest right in his human experience, his mind would be open to that subject.

The same principle can operate in real estate. Instead of seeking prospects among men and women and directing the sales approach to them, we would view it in the light that "man, whose breath is in his nostrils" does not make the decision as to whether he should buy or sell, even in such a matter as his own home. The decision rests with that divine intelligence which is love, and that intelligence would express Itself through the individual and lead him to his rightful decision.

In being reborn of the Spirit, we would come into agreement not only that the mind of us is God but rather that the mind of man is God, so instead of making our appeal to man, we would be realizing the mind of God as the intelligence of individual being.

Other Examples of Relying on the Inner Substance

A court case is a further example of the principle of the one Life expressing as the life of every individual. If we had to go to court, while we certainly would take every human footstep in the right direction, instead of our looking for justice and truth from judges, juries, attorneys, and witnesses, we would place our faith in the truth that God is the mind of man, that God is the source of wisdom, intelligence, love, and all the qualities we would like to find in a court of law. We do not expect the judge to render a decision but expect the decision to come from God through a judge, but always from God. We do not look to a man for justice.

If we go to a bank to borrow money, instead of wondering whether the banker got up on the right foot that morning and will be willing to grant the loan, we should have developed the state of consciousness in which we know that the banker is only the mediator between God and us. If there is a normal, natural, and rightful use for that loan, the banker must be God's agent in making the loan. If it should be divine wisdom to refuse the loan, so be it. Many a time a banker will make a loan when it is not divine wisdom for us to borrow, and then after we have borrowed we have difficulty in trying to repay the loan. In that case divine wisdom may prevent the granting of the loan.

No matter what occurs to us in our outer experience, we are surely approaching one of the highest levels of spiritual realization when we come to the agreement that it must be the activity of divine consciousness.

Freedom Through Desirelessness

In order that we may please God or call ourselves sons of God, it becomes necessary that the spirit of God, the consciousness of God, dwell in us. How can the spirit of God dwell in us unless we keep our mind stayed on God instead of on the things of the world? How can we develop a spiritual sense while we are still attempting to use truth to gain more of the world's goods instead of turning within to let the word of God manifest or express as the necessary things of our existence?

If we are ill at ease, in discomfort or pain, let us not search within for the error, but search within for the answer and for the truth. At once it is revealed that our heart is set on some thing or some one instead of being poised within. There truly is a rest, a peace, when the mind is free of all desire except the desire to realize God. Does this withdrawal from outer longings or this desire to realize God separate us from our good? On the contrary, to him whose mind is stayed on God there comes a rest from the dissatisfaction and unhappiness of the world, and a feast of joyous peace is spread before us out in the world. Even a table is set before us in the presence of our enemies. We withdraw from the senses all desire for change, correction, or adjustment in the affairs of the world and let the soul be at peace within, even resting from the desire for God. Thus, the world is overcome and His kingdom is come on earth to us.

At first that sounds as if it were so entirely transcendental, so completely spiritual, as to be out of the range of possibility for us. But it is not. It brings with it no violent change in the outer world. It does not mean running away to a monastery or convent or even taking a vacation in the hills for forty days. It means taking a vacation from the concern, the worry, the fear, and the doubt of the external world and attaining the ability to sit quietly for a few moments at a time with the mind refusing to entertain the world's problems. Even if it is only for a few minutes, we drop our desires and our concerns.

> My eyes are closed, and there is
> no world for me out here at this moment.
> There is nothing but this consciousness of peace
> and love within my own being.
> I have no concern for the outer world.
> I am not going to permit myself
> to think of friends or family,
> or of helping anyone
> or even accepting in my thought
> anyone to be helped. I am staying right here within
> my own being. Here I am, Father, You and I.

We have left the world outside in this communion between the Father, that deep Infinite Invisible, and the Son, the person we know as ourself, our family, friend, or enemy. In that communion with the Father within, there is no concern for the world, no concern for tomorrow.

Are We Willing to Pay the Price?

In the beginning this is not too easy, but the fact that it is not easy does not mean that it is not possible. It does not mean that we cannot achieve it. All the problems of the world want to crowd in, and we will have to make some effort because there is nothing on the spiritual path that is accomplished with ease. There is no wide and easy path. It is a straight and narrow one. When the Master said, "Strait is the gate, and narrow is the way, which leadeth unto life, and few there be that find it,"[4] he meant that only a few achieve it because most persons are not willing to pay the price. As the Master pointed out, one has a father-in-law; another one has something else to do; and one has to go and bid farewell to his family.[5] Many are bidden to the feast but few come.

Jesus' answer to these excuses was, "No man, having put his hand to the plough, and looking back, is fit for the kingdom of God."[6] When Jesus tells us that, he is telling us something about our own experience. We sit in the silence and either begin to worry about our landlord and how he is going to get his rent from us, or we begin to be concerned with the health of some of our friends or relatives whom we would like to see made whole. The fact that they are not making the same effort for themselves that we are making for them does not seem to enter our thought. We are determined that they are going to be well.

Whether it is the burying of the father-in-law or whether it is the concern for mother, father, sister, or brother, the Master reminded us that there must come a time when we leave mother, father, sister, brother for *My* sake. Our moments of silent meditation are that. It does not mean to desert our family. The Master never included in his teaching such a thing as deserting our duty or neglecting our responsibility to our loved ones.

The purpose of this work is to overcome the world, not improve it, but overcome it. So in our periods of silence, we might as well begin to overcome the world within our own being by dropping concern for it and having our moments of communion with the Father within. Soon, something happens in our meditation. After we acquire the ability to leave the world with all its worries and troubles outside and find this inner peace, there comes with it also an unfoldment from within that in one form or another assures us of God's presence.

Losing Concern

It is brought out in the twenty-third Psalm, "Yea, though I walk through the valley of the shadow of death, I will fear no evil: for thou art with me."[7] We would have no concern going about our tasks during the day, nor would we have any fears or doubts, if we had the assurance that God was with us on this journey. So this meditation results in an active and an actual realization of God's presence. We still may have some difficulty during the day. We still may have some mental or moral faults to be overcome, or financial problems to meet. We may have difficulties in human relationships and in our relationships with family, friends, or community. But these are no longer of the same importance since now we are consciously aware that God is with us. We have been given the assurance in one way or another:

I am with you; I am on the field.
"I will never leave thee, nor forsake thee."[8]
Even if you go through trials and tribulations,
fire and water, I will be with you.

That assurance is the word of God to which the Master referred when he said that we do not live by bread alone but by every word of God. Immediately there comes a lessening of personal responsibility. When that comes, we are entering the life of spiritual consciousness, because true spiritual consciousness is a life from which the personal sense of "I" has been eliminated.

True spiritual life is the life in which we can say, "I have no desires. I have no fear. I have no ambitions. I have no hopes. I have no concern. I have no will." It is a state of life in which the word "I" is transformed, and it becomes either Thou or the Father. So we do not ask what we should do about this, but rather, "Let's see what the Father is doing about it." Then we become aware of the Father's decision, the Father's activity, the Father's concern, and the Father's help.

If I say that we lose all ambition, I do not mean that we become ne'er-do-wells. I mean that we lose a *personal sense of ambition,* and our lives become the fulfillment of God's will and God's direction in us. Then we can truthfully say, not merely at our Gethsemane, not merely when it is a matter of life or death, but in every instance of our life: "Nevertheless not my will, but thine, be done."[9]

The Difference Between Saying and Hearing, "I Am Spiritual"

In a truly spiritual life, we never make statements such as "I am spiritual," or "I am the son of God," or "I am perfect," or "I am harmonious," or "I am rich." The word "I" should be used in spiritual matters, only when it refers to God. If we hear the voice within us say, "I will never leave thee, nor forsake thee," we are not saying, "I am spiritual." That is the word of God, "the still small voice,"[10] coming to us. If we hear such statements as "Be not afraid, I am with you," or, "Be still, and know that I am God,"[11] it is the Word welling up from within.

How many metaphysicians walk about with eyeglasses, hearing aids, leaning on crutches, or with some other problem saying, "Be still, and know that I am God," and believe that as human beings they really are. When we hear the still small voice within us telling us to "be still, and know that I am God," it really means that God has made Itself visible, tangible, and recognizable to you and me, and from then on we really know, "I and the Father are one, but the Father is greater than I. The kingdom of God is within me." After that, however, we will never make such statements as "I am Spirit," or "I am God," or "I am life eternal." Instead we will always be alert with that ear open to hear the voice say, *"I* am life eternal, and *I* will never leave you or forsake you."Then we will know that our life is infinite, eternal, and immortal.

The word "I" is given up more and more and drops out of our vocabulary, except in those moments when we hear it spoken to us within our own being. But the I that is the human being, that I drops away, and the person becomes a beholder of the activity of God, becomes a vehicle or an instrument through which or as which God acts. All responsibility is on His shoulder. There is no further personal responsibility. It is recognized that whatever activity comes forth during our day is the activity of God in operation. If it seems right and necessary today that we arrange a loan at the bank, it is important that the Father has instructed us to seek that loan, and that the Father takes care of it when it is due or secures a postponement for us.

Inadequacy of the Personal Sense of "I"

As long as we think out from the standpoint of "I," of how can I explain this away, how can I get this adjustment, or how can I get these people to see reason, just that long we are still dealing with material sense, and the responsibility rests on our shoulder. That is the reason we sometimes have success and sometimes failure, more often failure. The personal sense of I is never really adequate to the demands that the world makes upon it. But as we are able to close our eyes in meditation, drop that word "I" except in the sense, "Here I am Father, listening and communing," and let that assurance come, then when we open our eyes and go about our business, we no longer have to say: What shall I do next? Where will I go next? Instead we have an inner listening attitude as much as to say, "Father where do *we* go from here? What do *we* do next? What is Thy will?" That brings us to the ultimate of spiritual existence while still being in this world, in it, but not of it. We are still friends with one another; we are still husbands, wives, children, brothers, or sisters. We fulfill our functions on earth, but we fulfill them from the standpoint of our spiritual destiny, not our material concept of existence.

The entire spiritual life is a life of renunciation and, because of this, many persons have the idea that that means a life of poverty, of not having enough to eat, of not living in the right place, or of not having any possessions. That is not the meaning of renunciation. Renunciation means renouncing the personal sense of I. In proportion as we are able to renounce the personal sense of I, and the spirit of God, the consciousness of truth and love, the awareness of infinite power dwells in us, we are the children of God. We have overcome the fleshly sense of life. Our ambitions and desires are no longer on the forms of good, but on the cause of good which is the Father within. With that understanding, the forms appear in their due order and in the right way, always abundantly.

The Assurance of Divine Guidance

Every activity of our existence can be carried out under divine guidance. While we will all probably make mistakes from time to time, we can reduce the amount and seriousness of our mistakes more than ninety per cent by developing the habit of not doing anything until we have turned within for guidance or for the reassurance of the presence. We may not receive instruction as to how to do, what to do, or when to do it, but that is not necessary as long as we have the assurance, "*I* am with you." When we have the awareness of God's presence, then we know that we have spiritual power, divine intelligence, all power with us in whatever we are doing. Even if we humanly made a mistake, it would be corrected.

The point that I am making is that if we seek guidance in our human affairs, while dwelling on the human affairs, we may not and most likely will not get it. Only as thought is withdrawn from the problem, from the person, or from the condition, so that the soul is able to be at complete rest within our being and the mind has withdrawn its concern for the things of the world, are we given the assurance of divine guidance. After that as we return to the world of human affairs, we are spiritually led to think the right thoughts, to say the right words, and to take the right action.

We do not take the problem or the person into our silent meditation, but make an effort to have our periods of meditation in which the soul within is completely at rest from all thought of person and thing. When the outer world impinges on our thought, then the reminder comes, "Is this my affair or is it the affair of the Father within?" While we are concerned about that little "I" in relation to an external affair, we are still in the material sense of existence.

Let us suppose we are looking for a new location for the center of a spiritual activity. As long as the word "I" is involved in it, we may not be divinely led to the right place. When concern arises about the location, then the inner response comes, "Yes, but what is that to me? That can't be my problem. That must be God's problem, because this isn't my center: it is God's center. It is a place for the activity of Truth." So we might as well be consistent and recognize, if it is not our center but a place for the activity of Truth, why not let Truth lead us to it, and drop any sense of "I" doing it.

The same principle of letting God make every decision applies to where we live, whether we should buy or sell our home. Again the response must come, "What has that to do with me? This is God-maintained universe, a God-sustained and a God-governed universe, and I hope, I want to be, and I am aiming at being a God-governed individual. Therefore, there is no "I" to be concerned as to where or when or how. That is

God's problem and It must tell me the how, the when, the why, and the how much. I am not involved in any decision: God is involved in that. Let the government be on His shoulder.

We must maintain that truth in our consciousness day in and day out, and refuse to be tempted with that word "I." This has nothing to do with a person; this has to do with God's government of His universe. Then, whereas we may have been thinking of one neighborhood as against another neighborhood, when we have dropped that concept, we may be moved to the other end of the world. In every experience of so-called human existence in which we can learn to drop the concern we may have as to the outcome or refuse to permit the personal sense of I to enter into it, we have an experience leading to our spiritual demonstration.

We Cannot Bring God
to a Human Problem

I cannot repeat too often that failure comes directly from the attempt to bring God or Spirit into a human problem. It cannot be done because to God there are no human problems. To God there is no material universe. To say, "Oh, why doesn't God heal me?" is useless. In the kingdom of God, there is nothing to be healed and no one to be healed, but we will never know that until we leave the realm of physical existence and attain a soul-quietness. Then what we have been calling some discord in the physical body is not that at all. The body is a spiritual vehicle of life, a spiritual formation of life. It will not be that to us, however, while we are entertaining a concept of it in our thought as a physical structure, needing change, alteration, healing, or improvement.

So, too, as long as we think of our business as a human activity, needing more capital, more sales, more or better personnel, there is no way to bring the government of God into that business. There is only one way to bring the government of

God into our business, and that is the ability to sit down, shut out of our mind any thought of business, and begin to realize:

> This is a spiritual universe,
> and the activity of this universe is on God's shoulder.
> God can, through what we call natural laws,
> govern crops and tides
> and sun and moon and stars,
> so it must be possible
> for God to govern our business.
> Since "the earth is the Lord's and the fulness
> thereof,"[12] there can be no such thing as my business;
> there can be only God's business.

> I release this "I," "me," and "mine,"
> this personal sense of business.
> The only business is God-governed,
> and I am an onlooker, observing how
> beautifully God governs His business
> when I turn the business over to Him.

As we learn to become the onlooker, what we in the Infinite Way call the beholder, then we see the activity of God come through even into what we call our business.

Live as a Witness to God in Action

Every phase of our existence would be harmonious if we could step about six inches to the right of ourselves and watch the activity of God morning, noon, and night, or step a few inches in back of ourselves and watch the activity of God as it functions, instead of jumping in with the personal sense of I. The moment we come in with that word "I," we are running the business; we are doing something about health; we are trying to govern the universe; and in that degree we are living a material existence—sometimes good, more often not. We must watch our use of the word "I." The word "I" is always a devil, except when it is a word we hear in the ear. Every time we voice the word "I," we are voicing that devil of a selfhood apart from God, a sense of separateness.

A human being cannot heal, but the Lord God almighty in the midst of him can. And if he can open his ear, open his consciousness, so that the presence and power of God can be made visible and manifest, It will open the Red Sea; It will make manna fall from the sky; It will make the sins and diseases of the body disappear. No human being can do that, but the presence of God appearing as a person can. The person must get out of the way, let his consciousness be the arena, and let the activity of God do the work.

The work is done in the silence, which is the major part of all treatment even if we use the first half that is outlined above. Our work is not finished until we have completed the second half which is becoming quiet and resting in the Word. When the voice of God comes, and it may not be a voice, just a sensing of the presence of God, our footsteps do not falter or stray. The ill health, the lack, and limitation cannot remain because there cannot be the presence of God *and* error. If there is error or discord in our experience, we have not a conscious awareness of the presence of God. There is only one way in which we will attain that: silence, silence. We must be still and let the presence of God come through.

Whatever it is that appears as evil to our sense represents the human misconception or misperception of that which is divine. When dynamite was invented, it was not intended to be used for gunpowder. It was invented as a blasting instrument to take out big roots of trees or move huge rocks. It was man's misuse of dynamite that brought forth gunpowder. When atomic force was experimented with, it was not expected to be used for destructive purposes but to furnish energy for the industry of the world. Years and years ago, before atomic power was a reality, it was forecast that one thimbleful of it would carry an ocean liner to Europe and back for an entire year's trip. That was the hope of atomic power. But we have misused these things. This misuse has nothing to do with God. The substance of all form is God, even of atomic power. It is our misuse of it and misperception that causes the evils.

It is like money. There is nothing evil about money. It is our hugging and clutching it to ourselves as if it were supply, as if it were necessary for existence, that is the problem. In the same way there is nothing wrong with human love. What is wrong is the false sense of love, the misuse and abuse of it.

There is nothing wrong with any phase of human existence except man's perverted use of the divine energies, the divine wisdom, and the divine powers on earth. God is the substance of all form and everything that is, is beautiful and harmonious, only let us not pervert its use.

It is only a sense of separation from God that produces the discords and inharmonies of our existence. In the degree we understand that God is individual life, individual mind, individual soul, we can drop our concern for the personal sense of life, and life then flows harmoniously.

TAPE RECORDED EXCERPTS
Prepared by the Editor

On November 4, citizens of the United States have the opportunity and privilege of voting for their choice for the next President of the United States, a privilege they have had for so long that many have taken lightly and have failed to avail themselves of this opportunity.

Let us accept this opportunity as a solemn commitment and enter into it prayerfully, seeking inner guidance and knowing the spiritual identity, not only of the candidates but of every voter that each one may be an instrument for the divine government. "Eternal vigilance is the price of liberty."

Accepting the Responsibilities of Citizenship

"Let no one find in your consciousness condemnation. This does not mean that you do not have opinions. You are perhaps more firmly established in your opinion, if you have spiritual wisdom than would otherwise be the case. This does not mean being foolish and saying, 'What difference does it make who governs our country or what kind of a congress we have. Let anybody get in there because they're all spiritual.' That is really stupidity.

"If we have a clear consciousness of man's true identity, it will be pointed out to us who comes nearest to approaching that, in and for that particular position. . . . Just as we are guided to each other as patients and practitioners, students and teachers, just so we are guided to vote for the right candidate, the right party at any given time. . . .

"You and I, as citizens of a country, must fulfill our obligations as citizens. . . . As citizens, we have functions to perform. We have to render unto Caesar the things that are Caesar's. We cannot run and hide our heads and say, 'I will not fulfill my duty as a citizen. But I'll let you go out, my neighbor, and do it for me.' No, in whatever way is necessary, we are called upon to accept our responsibilities as citizens. We may not always agree with our governments and with what they are doing; we may not always agree that they are in the right. But one thing we cannot do is shirk the responsibility that comes to us as citizens. . . .

"Even while we are rendering unto Caesar the things that are Caesar's, even while we are obeying the law of the land in service, whether in paying taxes or serving in the army, even while we are doing that and knowing the wrongness of it humanly, we can be about our special business of prayer, of bringing the realization of the kingdom of God to earth through our consciousness. We can be helping to settle the affairs of the world, not by might and not by power but by the spirit of God. While we today are in the midst of the turmoil, the result of which no one can foresee with any degree of accuracy, even while we know that humanly we are so little, so unimportant to this world. . . nevertheless we can be a bigger power than the man who built the atom bomb. . . .

"God is the only righteous one. . . the only good one. If we are sufficiently nothingness, the spirit of God can function through us. You have no way of knowing who the individual is, or where or when, who may be. . . awakened out of his 'Saulness' into 'Paulness.' . . . None of us has any idea who may be reached by the Christ and see the light and be in a position behind the affairs of the world where that influence can throw the situation on to the side of spiritual power. . . . It is not a person who is going to come forth with an idea to save this world. It is the Christ; and the individual in the right place, at the right time, with a degree of receptivity will be the individual through whom the solution will appear to come. . . . Your function and mine is to be an instrument through which the presence of God can touch humanity. . . . We have no way of knowing the degree of power that is in one individual consciously realizing the presence of God."

Joel S. Goldsmith, "Grace,"
The 1958 London Advanced Class, Tape 3:1.

"The Christ is the solution, not the first coming of the Christ, not the second coming of the Christ, or the third coming, just the coming of the Christ to individual consciousness, and the coming of the Christ cannot be described or analyzed or dissected. The coming of the Christ means an inner grace,... An assurance within that He that is within you is greater than he that is in the world."

Joel S. Goldsmith, "The Way,"
The 1960 Chicago Open Class, Tape 3:1.

Chapter Nine

Seek the Substance,
Not the Form

The world seeks to find peace, joy, satisfaction, supply, home, or companionship in people and things. But the Master said, "My kingdom is not of this world."[1] So the purpose of our work is to turn away from the way of the world to the spiritual way. In turning to the spiritual path, we learn that the world's weapons, its manner of protecting itself and its way of seeking its good, will not do for us.

"The kingdom of God is within you."[2] If we think of that literally, it immediately becomes clear why there is no use going outside ourselves to find our good, that is, not if the kingdom of God is within us. The place to seek our good must necessarily be within. The spiritual revelators of all time agree on this truth, and they have been able to teach their immediate disciples or students how to make contact with that withinness and, because of making this inner contact, they have been able to lead a life without struggle or strain, a life of harmony and peace.

The disciples of these spiritual revelators seem to have had difficulty in passing that principle on to those of the next generation, and those who followed experienced much the same difficulty, so that a spiritual teaching has thrived principally during the immediate lifetime of its revelator and to a lesser degree in the following generation or two. In the case of the Master, his ministry lasted for about 300 years before it died out and all but vanished from the earth, probably longer than any of those of which we have knowledge.

The Spread of
Spiritual Teaching and Healing

Since that time there have been individual mystics who have caught the vision of withinness and have had the usual experience of some measure of success with their immediate disciples and for a short while afterwards. From the 12th to the 17th century, reaching all the way from Switzerland to England, there were mystics with large followings who had attained the spiritual vision. But unfortunately throughout that period the established church persecuted these religious teachings to such an extent that by the 17th century they had all practically been wiped off the earth.

Today in a revival of mysticism we are living in a climate of greater freedom. In the first place, since the last appearance on earth of spiritual or mystical teachings, the largest and the most esteemed nations on earth have sanctioned freedom of religious worship so that there is no direct persecution of spiritual teachings either from the church or from the state. There have been a few minor attempts at persecution but, in a considerable part of the world, there is a greater degree of freedom so the spiritual life can be practiced without fear of outside persecution.

The second transition that has taken place is that men have learned that it is not necessary to fight the church or tear it down. Since, for the most part, the church is not attempting to limit religious freedom, there is no reason to do away with it. Through the gradual process of evolution eventually the church itself will be embracing and presenting to the world increasingly deeper teachings concerning the spiritual life. That has already happened in one of the large Protestant churches in England that has sanctioned spiritual healing and has even set aside funds for their ministers to study spiritual healing and spiritual teachings.

In the United States, too, a friendly attitude toward spiritual healing has developed. In the better relationship that exists among those of a religious bent, there is a higher understanding of the purpose, not only of spiritual teaching, but a higher understanding of the true nature and function of the church. In some cases, practically the entire membership of certain churches is opening itself to spiritual teaching, bringing the world very close to an era of spiritual good. It is coming upon us more rapidly than any of us can know.

Becoming Acquainted with God

Spiritual living is based, not on the observance of forms, ceremonies, or creeds, but on the ability to contact God. There is God, and not only is there God, but there is a God at hand, "closer. . . than breathing, and nearer than hands and feet."[3] And the Master tells us that the kingdom of this God is within us.

Since there is a God, it becomes necessary that you and I know this God. "Acquaint now thyself with him, and be at peace: thereby good shall come unto thee."[4] "In all thy ways acknowledge him, and he shall direct thy paths."[5] "And this is life eternal, that they might know thee the only true God."[6] If you are not experiencing life eternal, understand once and for all that you do not know God. If you are not enjoying the harmony, the peace, and the prosperity to which you are entitled as children of God, then acknowledge that you have not made this acquaintanceship. To become acquainted with God and to know God is to have all your ways directed by Him, to be kept in peace, and to receive the blessing of life eternal, life harmonious, in short, the good life.

"Yet Have I Not Seen the Righteous Forsaken, Nor His Seed Begging Bread"

After I became involved in the healing work, success came to me very quickly and with it a goodly amount of prosperity. But shortly thereafter I moved to another city and took upon myself larger obligations. Outwardly it seemed as if I had made a mistake because, while I continued to be very successful in the healing work, I was very unsuccessful in demonstrating supply. I found myself with a severe problem of lack and limitation, trying to maintain a family on an insufficient income. I was doing beautiful healing work, being engaged in it all day and all night, and yet I did not have a sufficient return to keep the wheels of commerce greased.

For two years I had been in the healing work and not only were physical healings taking place, but the problem of supply was being met for many of those I was helping. Yet here was my own personal problem of lack. You can imagine that I could not rest until I knew the answer to that. It probably was not necessary that I eat, drink, or be clothed, but it was necessary that I know how to meet this problem for the sake of those who were trusting in the degree of my realization.

On one particular day, while walking along the street on my way to my office, the thought came to me that if I really knew God this could not be happening. I believed the Bible when it said, "I have been young, and now am old; yet have I not seen the righteous forsaken, nor his seed begging bread."⁷ So it must be there was not any fault with God, or Truth, but that the fault must lie with me. Evidently I was not righteous in the correct sense. Evidently I did not have the right idea of supply. Something surely was wrong.

The unfoldment was clear that it must be because of my lack of understanding. God was not responsible for this situation. At first glance it would seem impossible for a person to be actively engaged in spiritual work and be the instrument for bringing about healings of every kind and still not know God or have the correct understanding of God. Yet I thought it must be true, because scripture is true. The fault was entirely with me, and it must be that I did not know God.

Quotations About God Are Not God

I decided to test this and find out whether or not I knew God. I asked myself what God is. Then I began to give all the answers that you would probably be giving in your mind if you had been asked that question. Quickly I realized that the answers I was giving could not be truth because all I was doing was quoting: "God is love."[8] John said that. I did not know it. "God is law." Somebody else said that, but I did not know it.

So I quickly realized that whatever I knew about God was not a realization about God. My knowledge of God consisted of quotations about God, quotations describing what other people knew about God, nothing that I knew. When it came right down to it, I knew nothing about God but quotations. I did not know God. And there is a great difference between knowing God and knowing statements of truth about God. It is quite a different thing.

What Am I?

When I pondered the subject of what God is and what I knew about God, no answer came. I began to think about man and my idea of what man is and what I am. It was a long walk, but during that walk I realized that God is the *I* of my being, the *I Am,* not my humanhood, not my personal mind or powers of understanding, but the *I Am* of me, the very *I* or spiritual Selfhood of me. God constitutes that; God is that.

God is the very life, the very soul, the very consciousness of individual man. God is the mind of individual man. If that is true, then all the intelligence God has is the intelligence of man.

All that the Father has is mine. All of the God-mind is my mind; all of the God-soul is my soul; all of the God-spirit is my spirit; all of the God-supply is my supply; all of the God-love is my love, because I and the Father are one, and all that the Father has is mine. It is that oneness that constitutes the infinity of individual being.

In and of myself, I would be nothing, but since God constitutes my real being and is the Father of my real being, then God has established the fullness of His wisdom in me, the fullness of His love, the fullness of His life, and the fullness of His supply in me. "The earth is the Lord's, and the fulness thereof,"[9] and "Son, thou art ever with me, and all that I have is thine."[10] That immediately changed the situation; that changed my understanding; that changed my life. Now came the realization that since this allness constitutes individual being, my good does not have to come to me from outside: it has to come from inside.

Releasing Our Good from Within

God has a way of meeting our need at every level, and so it was not long after that unfoldment came when I ran across Browning's poem explaining that you must not try to open an entry for good to come to you from without but rather you must open out away for the imprisoned splendor to escape from within. In other words, all good is within you: all of eternity, immortality, all of Godhood, all of Christhood, all of spirituality is embodied within you. But you must open out away for it to escape.

Watch the miracle that takes place in your life as you realize that this splendor of God—this infinite love, this infinite life, this divine wisdom, this spiritual grace, the Comforter—is already within you. This that multiplies loaves and fishes, that heals the sick, that preaches the gospel to the poor, that opens the eyes of the blind is already within you. Even when you are reading books of spiritual wisdom, you must remember not to try to add spiritual power or spiritual truth to yourself, but rather to read for a further understanding that all of this is already contained within you.

Such an understanding changes your mode of life. You no longer look outside to persons. A wife immediately loses the feeling that she is dependent on her husband. A husband immediately loses the sense that he is dependent on his position, his investments, or his business. Each one comes to the realization that even though supply may come through those channels, and they are all legitimate, the source of supply is within one's self.

In the realization of that, new and larger avenues open and the fear that in case one avenue should be closed no others would be opened disappears, because in the realization that all of this is within one's self it can open anew every single day.

Forms of Supply

Outwardly supply takes many forms, the forms of money, food, clothing, housing, transportation, capital in business, and many others. These are the forms, but supply itself is not a form. Supply itself is never felt with human fingers. Supply is never heard or tasted. Supply is Spirit, and supply is within you; it is never visible; and it never becomes visible.

You behold in the outer world the forms that supply assumes, but the supply itself you never see, and that is why, like Moses,[11] you can realize that you do not have to live on yesterday's manna, nor do you have to pick manna for tomorrow because supply is infinite and supply is omnipresent wherever you may be. You will never see it, so you will never have any evidence of it insofar as your eyesight is concerned. Through spiritual discernment, you will have to understand that this is true. Later you will see the proof of it, not by ever seeing supply, but by seeing the *forms* which supply assumes.

So it is with truth. You will never see or hear truth. Truth is invisible and inaudible. You may read about truth and you may hear the symbols of truth, but that is not truth. Truth Itself is within you, and that truth is Spirit; truth Itself is God. What you read in a book or what you hear with your ear, these are but the symbols of truth.

Symbols of Supply

Money is a symbol of supply. The fruit on the trees and the crops in the ground, these are symbols of supply, forms which supply assumes, but supply itself is invisible, and it is within you. In *The Infinite Way,* [12] there is the illustration of supply and the orange tree. It is brought out that oranges, even to the orange-grower, are not supply. When the oranges have been picked and sold, the wind has blown them away, or the crops have been destroyed by insects, the supply is still there because the supply is operating inside the tree and will appear in its due season as another crop of oranges. When that crop of oranges is taken away, the supply has not been used up because the form of supply is going to appear next season in another crop.

Many of you who have lived through two wars and a major depression as well as a few minor ones have known persons of wealth or abundance who have experienced lack and limitation—sometimes total lack. But often it was not too long before most of those same persons re-established themselves, sometimes with a greater degree of wealth than they originally had. Even in losing their money they did not lose their supply. They still had whatever was the cause of the abundance of the world's goods which they had accumulated, the same intelligence, energy, ideas, inspiration, or love. These qualities bring forth the forms of supply, but ideas, inspiration, intelligence, wisdom, service, and love are invisible. They are always invisible, although the forms are visible.

Often in the sale of a business there will be an item labeled "good will." In one such case, which could be multiplied many times over, a business sold its assets for half a million dollars but its good will for one million dollars. The intangible assets were worth more than the physical assets of the corporation. The good will, something that no one can ever see, hear, taste, touch, or smell, is an intangible.

Is this not also true with every poet, author, sculptor, painter, and composer? It is the invisible which is the substance of the visible. If they did not have a light, an inspiration, or an inner something, it would never have appeared outwardly as a poem, a book, a teaching, a painting, or any other form of art. If you can accept this, you will have received one of the most practical lessons you have ever had in life, because it will help you to stop trying to demonstrate supply.

Demonstrate God, Not the Forms

When you give up the attempt to demonstrate supply, you will find yourself in possession of abundance. That which you are trying to demonstrate is not supply. It is a *form* of supply, and after you have attained it, it is not permanent; you use it up and have to do the work of demonstrating it all over again. To have to demonstrate supply every week or every month makes of life a burdensome labor instead of experiencing the joy of fulfillment.

You have to demonstrate supply only once, and it rolls on forever making it unnecessary to take anxious thought for its forms. But if you demonstrate forms of supply, they break, they are eaten up, or they wear out, and then comes that old round of rent-day, clothes-day, holiday, and the need again for a new demonstration. Stop it now. Demonstrate supply itself once and for all, and then let that supply appear outwardly in its own way as form.

First of all, the way to demonstrate supply is to recognize that God is supply. You have to demonstrate God, and that is all. You have one demonstration to make, and that demonstration is the realization of God within you You have to demonstrate the consciousness of the presence of God. You have to demonstrate the awareness of God's presence. Once you have done that, the rest automatically follows. Every year, in due season, a new crop appears; every time new shoes are needed, they appear; every time an automobile is needed, it appears; every time the rent is due, it appears. Why? Because you have demonstrated Infinity.

It is possible to raise funds, to work for money or to borrow it, and some few people for a short while have succeeded in stealing it. That is not a demonstration of supply. Although the demonstration of supply will appear outwardly as some form of work or fruitful activity, the demonstration of supply is the demonstration of the realization of God. God is the source and fount of all supply.

When you have demonstrated God, you have the whole source of supply, the multiplier of loaves and fishes, the multiplier of all the crops on the trees and in the ground. You have but one demonstration to make, and that is the demonstration of God. You cannot make that demonstration anywhere outside your own consciousness. It is not something external to you. It is not an experience external to you. It is an experience that takes place within your own consciousness.

Seek the Substance
of Health or Eternality

Demonstrating supply is like demonstrating eternality. Once you demonstrate eternality all you have to do is let the clock tick off the minutes, and as the minutes are going by you will be moving toward infinity, but you have nothing to do with time. You do not demonstrate time and you do not demonstrate youth. Nobody can demonstrate youth; nobody can demonstrate himself one day younger than he is. But you can demonstrate life eternal. The way to do that is to demonstrate God, because God is life eternal. So when you demonstrate God you demonstrate life eternal.

Health, too, is an experience of consciousness. Eventually you will stop the attempt to demonstrate health, because you will not succeed permanently. You can demonstrate an individual healing sometimes, but that is not health because the next week or the next month the same thing or some other thing can return, indicating that you have not demonstrated health. If you had demonstrated health, health would be a continuous experience. You have merely demonstrated an individual healing, and sometimes not even that.

When you decide you no longer want to demonstrate health, but you want to demonstrate the awareness of God who is the health of your countenance, you have demonstrated health and wholeness, not merely a physical healing. When you have such an experience, it is far beyond a mere healing: you have demonstrated your unchanging health, the continuity of the health and harmony of body. Separate and apart from the demonstration of the presence of God, however, it cannot be accomplished. You can be healed physically by a doctor; you can be healed mentally; but you cannot demonstrate health that way. You demonstrate health through demonstrating the presence of God.

Having God you have all that belongs to God: "Son, thou art ever with me, and all that I have is thine." As long as you are with God and God is with you, you have supply, all that the Father has. That will appear externally as health, as money, transportation, or any other thing of which you have need.

How to Demonstrate the Presence of God

The demonstration of God will prove to be the most practical experience in your whole life. In reality, there is no enduring practicality in anything but the demonstration of God. Regardless of how practical things attained by human means

may seem to be, it is far more practical to have achieved the realization of God, and then be able to reiterate with conviction
Paul's statement, "I live; yet not I, but Christ liveth in me."[13]

> "I can do all things through Christ
> which strengtheneth me."[14]
> The Christ is my wisdom.
> The Christ within me is the presence and power
> that goes before me to
> "make the crooked places straight."[15]

Assuming that the way of a life of harmony, peace, and
abundance is demonstrating the consciousness of God's presence, an awareness of God's presence, a realization of God, or
demonstrating a God-experience, how do you achieve it? The
reading and study of the correct letter of truth is a step in that
direction. The hearing of truth is another step. It has been discovered that reading books of truth in which the principles of
spiritual living and healing are set forth is one way toward realization. Hearing truth may be even better for some than reading it, but reading it and hearing it together tend to result in
miracles of understanding.

Meditation Unlocks the Door of Understanding

There is a third step that is greater than the first two and yet
dependent on the first two. When you have heard or read the
word of truth and have it within your consciousness, meditation
brings it to life. Meditation brings the experience to a focus, that
is, to an actual realization. After reading and hearing about the
principles, the practice of meditation is the most important
activity in your life. Reading and hearing alone may lead you to
the awareness of God, but meditation will shorten the time by
ninety percent. Meditation is one of the most powerful means
ever discovered of attaining God-realization.

Meditation takes your thought entirely away from the outside world and brings it within yourself where the kingdom of God is. Within yourself is where you will have to find God. Since a God-experience is an activity of your consciousness and has to be experienced through your consciousness, when you are within yourself, within your own consciousness, you are at that point where the experience can take place, that is, where the demonstration of God takes place. It never takes place outside your being.

How should you meditate? In every one of the Infinite Way writings, there is at least one chapter on meditation, prayer, or communion, three subjects which really embrace the meditation process. In almost every one of the tape recordings you will hear a meditation, in fact some of the recordings consist of a solid hour of meditation. Through these, you will be brought into the actual meditation. Such recorded lessons go further than teaching you how to meditate. They can often bring about within you a taste or touch of God-consciousness.

Opening a Person to the God-Experience

In all Infinite Way literature much is written of healing: mental, moral, and financial, as well as physical healing. Do not be mistaken, however, and believe that the purpose of the Infinite Way is just to heal your body. Nothing could be further from the truth. Healing your body as such is of little interest to practitioners. Their interest is in opening an individual to the God-experience because inevitably health follows. It is impossible to commune with God without that communion taking the form of better health, more abundant supply, a more stable temperament, and a better character. The very presence of God is a purifying agency.

It is right, natural, and normal to have health, and even physical health is usually better than disease, although disease can be more conducive to spiritual awakening. Healthy people very seldom turn to the study of God, more especially if they are not only healthy but have adequate supply. They are so completely taken care of on the outer plane that they feel no need to turn to God. Many times people have said, "Oh yes, I know it must be a wonderful thing to know God, and when I am older I am going to turn to God, but I have no need of Him right now. I am healthy; I am young; and I have plenty of supply." Most persons turn to God in their own incompleteness, whether it is incompleteness in health, supply, or human relationships. They wonder if God can do something for them. So it is that very often physical discomfort is the greatest ally of God.

Dominion over Fear-Thoughts

In the beginning while you are very much involved in this human experience, you are like an antenna and you feel world thoughts. If you are among people who have intense fear, all of a sudden you begin to feel a sense of fear within yourself and you are filled with fear. It is not you at all; you are absorbing a world-fear. When the newspapers are full of bad news, you may easily fall into a state of being fearful and being depressed, not realizing that you are reacting to the newspaper, TV, or radio headlines.

Sometimes, even though you do not read the news and do not hear the radio or television programs, nevertheless you are enough of an antenna to pick fear up out of the air and feel it. Through this work, you learn to protect yourself from that vulnerability so that you do not pick up the thoughts of others.

Among peoples of a primitive culture, over the centuries there has grown up a great superstition on the part of many of them which is a fear that somebody near or at a distance can think an evil thought and harm them. Traces of that can be found in the United States among many different people who grew up with a superstitious fear of other's thoughts and who have not come into enlightenment. We have some groups in the northeastern states, who have as part of their religious belief, a fear that they can be hexed or cursed. They live in fear of the enmity of a person, thinking that he will go to a hexer and have them hexed which means they will die, become very sick, never find their mate, or have some catastrophic experience.

Among the Hawaiians there were two groups of kahunas or priests: the good kahunas and the evil kahunas. The good kahuna was like a practitioner or spiritual teacher. A person could go to him for council, for guidance, health, prayers, healing, and for all manner of good. But on the other hand, if he wanted curses, he would manage somehow to get a hair of his enemy's head or a little piece of his fingernail, and take that to the evil kahuna. The evil kahuna would then get to work to put a curse on the enemy and the next day the enemy died. It actually worked, because the thing which that person feared had come upon him.

If you can be made to give sufficient power to hexers or bad kahunas, they can give you a hard time. In the same way, if you really believe that there are people on earth who can malpractice you, they can, but not through any power they have but because you have invested them with a power. You have accepted the belief and you suffer from your own belief. Never doubt that, for it is an absolute truth.

Nobody in the world has the power to malpractice you, nobody. Nobody has the power to cause any evil to appear in your experience. Nobody has the power to do a single harmful thing to you except that you give him permission; you invite him by entertaining a fear of a power outside your own being. The moment you begin to grasp the idea of God as the only power, never again will you fear the thoughts of an individual, a group of individuals, or a whole nation of individuals.

Dealing with Unruly Thoughts

Students, new to meditation, and some who have long unsuccessfully attempted meditation are beset by unruly thoughts, uncontrolled thoughts that run around in their mind. Their first effort is to stop this or get rid of such disturbing, distracting thoughts. They do not usually succeed.

Do not waste time trying to stop unruly or unwelcome thoughts that come into your mind when you meditate. Completely ignore them and go about your own business of doing what you have gone into meditation to do. If you want to meditate and there are a great many thoughts running through your mind—fear thoughts, sometimes thoughts of pain, sensuality—do not become angry with yourself for thinking thoughts that you do not like because it is not you thinking them. They are not your thoughts: they are world thoughts.

Becoming Unreceptive to World-Thoughts

When you are in meditation, the first temptation is either to fear or be so disgusted with these thoughts that you cannot keep them out of your head. You will be able to keep them out eventually, if in the beginning you will ignore them and not try to get rid of them or stop them. They are not your thoughts, and you can prove it within the next few minutes. When you go into meditation, say the word, "I," and then decide what you are going to think or ponder about God. You are going to take the word God into your consciousness and you are going to ask yourself: What do I know about God? What have I heard or read about God? What is it about God that is real to me, that I have confidence in, that I have knowledge of?

As you persist in that line of thought or introspection, these thoughts are still going to go on in your head, only you are not going to pay any attention to them. You will be able to carry on your contemplation of God even while those thoughts are moving around inside of you, and that alone will prove that your thoughts are subject unto you. These other thoughts are merely something that come and go, and when you have learned to persist in your contemplative meditation, eventually by starving out these thoughts, they go and never return again.

You must come to a place where you make yourself an instrument for God and do not permit yourself to be used as an instrument for the human mind or the universal beliefs of mankind. In other words, you should not be receptive or responsive to world-thoughts. If the people of the world want to think that the weather is bad and they may catch cold, or if they believe in the power of infection and contagion, you do not have to accept that. You can keep yourself free of world-beliefs by taking hold of yourself and agreeing consciously:

> I and the Father are one,
> and the activity of the Father is expressed in me
> and through me. God's wisdom,
> God's law, and God's love govern me, control me,
> and permeate my entire being.
> I am subject to divine grace alone.
> I am subject to God's kingdom. I am subject to God's
> laws. I am subject to the life of God.
> God permeates my being. God enfolds me.
> God governs, guides, maintains, and sustains me.
>
> I am an instrument of God.
> I show forth the handiwork of God.
> I show forth God's glory.
> I do not respond to world-beliefs.

You must consciously realize your freedom from world-beliefs. By having been born a human being, you are subject to good and evil; you are subject to truth and you are subject to error. A human being is a combination of good and evil, but in the son of God there is neither good nor evil: the son of God has only the pure spirit of God within himself—no opposites and no pairs of opposites. The transition into sonship must be made consciously by every individual. By birth you came into this experience. But the transition into spiritual sonship comes only as an individual experience and must be accomplished consciously, as a conscious act of your own being.

TAPE RECORDED EXCERPTS
Prepared by the Editor

"Now we are facing half a dozen human problems, not only in our national life but in our international life, any one, or two, or three of which could tear the foundations out from under our entire civilization. We have the opportunity, if we are willing to tackle the problem, of putting up that sword, of relinquishing our confidence, faith, or hope in any human administrations or human plans or human agreements. . . of no longer having faith in princes, potentates, or powers, but of actually retiring within ourselves for an assurance of an inner grace.

"The Christ is the solution, not the first coming of the Christ, not the second coming of the Christ, or the third coming, just the coming of the Christ to individual consciousness, and the coming of the Christ cannot be described or analyzed or dissected. The coming of the Christ means an inner grace, . . . An assurance within that He that is within you is greater than he that is in the world."

Joel S. Goldsmith, "The Way,"
The 1960 Chicago Open Class, Tape 3:1.

Chapter Ten

Start the Flow to God

Cast thy bread upon the waters:
for thou shalt find it after many days.
Ecclesiastes 11:1

For whosoever hath, to him shall be given,
and he shall have more abundance:
but whosoever hath not,
from him shall be taken away even that he hath.
Matthew 13:12

The earth is the Lord's, and the fulness thereof.
Psalm 24:1

Son, thou art ever with me,
and all that I have is thine.
Luke 15:31

The kingdom of God is within you.
Luke 17:21

The Spirit itself beareth witness with our spirit,
that we are the children of God:
And if children, then heirs; heirs of God,
and joint-heirs with Christ.

Romans 8:16,17

The above quotations indicate that you now have the fullness of the God-head bodily; you have all that God has. It may not appear that way looking out with the eyes, hearing with the ears, tasting, touching, or smelling with the physical senses. It may not appear at first to the physical senses that you have all that God has or even a little bit of it. It may even appear that you lack something. But you are not to judge by appearances. You are to judge righteous or spiritual judgment, and spiritual judgment, that is, spiritual discernment, reveals that all that God is you are. All that the Father has is yours. All that God is, you individually are.

Allness

The allness of God is made manifest as the allness of the son. God is both the Father and the Son: God, the Father, God, the Son. When you acknowledge your sonship, you are knowing the truth, and the truth will make you free, free from discordant appearances or experiences. But the truth you must know is that nothing can be added to you, that you cannot get anything, you cannot achieve anything, and you cannot demonstrate anything because all that the Father has is already yours.

The life of God is your life; therefore, your life is eternal. The mind of God is your mind; therefore, you have infinite intelligence. God, the Soul, is your individual soul; therefore, you are as pure as God. Outward appearances have nothing to do with it. Outward beliefs about yourself or others have nothing to do with it. Outward actions in contradiction to that have nothing to do with it. The truth of the matter is that God, the Father, is made evident as God, the Son, and you are that son of God. In your spiritual identity, you are the full Christ or son of God, endowed with the power to multiply loaves and fishes, heal the sick, raise the dead, and open the eyes of the blind.

The Christ-identity of every person is the son of God. The Christ is the Comforter. The Christ it is that multiplies loaves and fishes, heals the sick, raises the dead, preaches the gospel to the poor, and opens the eyes of the blind. That gift of Christhood is your true being. Your acknowledgment of this is knowing the truth that will make you free from human beliefs, appearances, theories, and rumors.

Acknowledge, "I Have"

When you acknowledge that you lack and have not, you have not only made this true for yourself today but much more true tomorrow, because from that moment the little that you have will be taken from you. When you say, "I haven't enough supply"; or "I haven't enough understanding," or when you even think such thoughts, you are on the way to losing what little you have.

If you have only as much as the disciples had when they had a few loaves and fishes and acknowledge that you have a few loaves and fishes, then the loaves and fishes will be multiplied. If, like the widow with the cruse of oil, you acknowledge that you have a few drops of oil, that oil will be multiplied. To declare that you have not enough, what you already have would truly prove to be an insufficiency. Had Jesus accepted the limitation of "but five loaves, and two fishes"[1] it would have been an insufficiency for the multitudes. But when the Master recognized what they already had, the multiplication began. You will never lack when you know:

The infinite wisdom of God is mine. All God's love is
mine. All immortality is already mine, all eternal life.
All of "my peace" is mine, for
"My peace I give unto you: not as the world giveth,
give I unto you,"² not just more money
or more health. That "my peace,"
a spiritual state of consciousness, which knows no
lack, limitation, or destruction, is mine.

Spiritual sonship is your true identity. Spiritual sonship
with all the fullness of its meaning is your true identity. In
spite of any appearances that may now engulf you, you must
know the truth of your relationship to God. You must know
the truth of your true identity as God manifest, God revealed,
God individualized, God expressed. That is your true identity.
The qualities of God, therefore, are the qualities of your individual being.

Reject the
Temptation to Accept Lack

If temptation appears as a lack of supply, lack of companionship, lack of health, you have to turn upon it: " 'Get thee
behind me, Satan.'³ Stop trying to tempt me to believe that I
am not the full and complete son of God. Get thee behind me,
for I know, regardless of appearances, that all the Father has is
mine. The very place whereon I stand is holy ground because
God is here. The allness, the fullness, and the fulfillment of
God are here where I am. Herein is God glorified that I bear
much fruit." That must always be your knowing of the truth
to the point of realization in spite of appearances that come to
tempt you.

Anyone can give way to temptation when called upon for
help and adopt an attitude of "I guess that's right. I haven't
enough understanding; I haven't enough wisdom; I haven't

enough spiritual power; I haven't enough dollars or pounds; I haven't enough companionship." Anyone can accept the appearance at face value, but not you who are a disciple of the Christ. You must follow the precepts of Christ Jesus and not do your alms in public; you must not pray for food, clothing, or housing; you must not take "thought for your life, what ye shall eat, or what ye shall drink; nor yet for your body, what ye shall put on."[4] "Your heavenly Father knoweth that ye have need of all these things."[5] God provided whatever is necessary for you in the beginning before time began, and it is now established in your consciousness.

Sharing Your I-Haveness

If you take the position of a human being to whom something must be added, you lose whatever little understanding you have. If you take your position on the divinity of your being and its fullness and completeness, instead of trying to demonstrate something to come to you, you begin to spend out from within yourself. You begin to share truth; you begin to share dollars, pounds, or shillings; you begin to share books; you begin to share companionship; or you begin to share service. Your sharing stems from knowing that since you already have this fullness and completeness within you, you can share it to whatever extent you permit it to flow from you.

When you take the position that you are the center through which God is flowing, there is no limitation to what you can give or share or be or do because you are claiming nothing of yourself. You are claiming the allness of God as the measure of your individual capacity. You do not begin by writing out a check for a million dollars, which amount you do not have in the bank. You begin by sharing one shilling or one dollar if that is the measure of today's capacity. Someday you may increase it to two, five, or ten until you arrive at the fullness of realization. If you know some truth, share that little truth with those who desire it, and only with those, knowing that even as you share it, it multiplies in you.

Spiritual Interpretation of Scripture,[6] Came Out of Sharing

When I was living in California, four couples came to me and asked, "Would you teach us what you know about the Bible?"

I said, "Certainly, come to my home some evening for an hour, and I will tell you all I know because I can tell you everything I know in one hour."

"Oh no, that's not true. You know something that we don't know."

"Look, please believe me, there are two statements in the Bible that I know, and only two. If there are any more, I am not aware of them, but those two statements are important."

One of those statements was "Cease ye from man, whose breath is in his nostrils, for wherein is he to be accounted of."[7] I knew that that meant to stop looking at mortal man and trying to heal him, improve him, or reform him. Instead, I was to leave him strictly alone, learn about spiritual identity, and mortal man will "die daily." That I knew. I knew, too, that "My kingdom is not of this world." I knew that this Christ-kingdom had nothing to do with the round of human activities and that I could know and enjoy the fruitage of the Christ-kingdom only as I rose above human sense. I could not draw It down into the human world, but if I drew It to myself, I would still be in the world, but not of the world.

Since those who asked for instruction on the Bible did not believe me, I said, "I'll tell you what we will do. I don't know why you want it; I don't know what it is you want because I really know very little about the Bible, but the month of April is coming. Suppose we take one night a week for four weeks. I can cover the whole Bible in those four evenings with an hour each evening."

A week before we were to begin, I sat down in my office, talked to God as if He were sitting at the other side of my desk, and said, "Father, look; what do these people want of me? You know that I don't know the Bible. You know that there is very little in it that I have ever understood, a few passages perhaps, but that's all. What is it that they want? I know You sent them but what for? I don't know what to give them. Now what is going to happen Friday night when we meet? Please, please tell me."

And I did a little begging and pleading. In all my writings I have said that you should not do that, but this sort of begging and pleading is a little different. This is when God and I get together in what seems like a very human way, and we talk just brother to brother, man to man. So I sat with the Bible in my hand, waiting, waiting, waiting, and finally I opened it to a place very close to the Ten Commandments. I leafed through that part of the Bible and decided to go back to the very beginning of Moses, read all the way through, and see if that was what God was trying to tell me.

As I read from the beginning of the life of Moses and through the Ten Commandments, all of a sudden something struck me as very strange. The Ten Commandments are not spiritual. How could any person tell a spiritual man not to steal, to honor his mother and father, or not to commit adultery? That is rather nonsensical, isn't it? You do not talk that way to spiritual people. There is nothing spiritual about this at all. Then it dawned on me, "The law was given by Moses, but grace and truth came by Jesus Christ."[9]

In the Old Testament, Moses sets forth laws governing good citizenship, the law under which men and women should live, but under the Christ we are no longer good men and women: we are spiritual beings. Jesus was revealing spiritual sonship. So our first lesson was that the Ten Commandments were just an attempt to make us better and more honorable human beings. I pointed out that the time must come, however, when we rise

above being merely good human beings into our spiritual identity in which we would be neither good nor bad: we would be
eternal, immortal, spiritual being.

Ruth and Naomi

The next Friday night came, and before that God and I got
together again for another "hair pulling" match, and this time
when I opened the book it was to the story of Ruth and Naomi.
As I read it through, I thought that that's a beautiful story but a
strange thing to give me: "Entreat me not to leave thee, or to
return from following after thee: for whither thou goest, I will
go; and where thou lodgest, I will lodge: thy people shall be my
people, and thy God my God."[10]
    I read it again and again until I caught its import. There
never was a Ruth: Ruth is the Christ in individual consciousness
that never leaves you, and when you have lost your family, your
fortune, and you are at the crossroads, not knowing which way
to go, the Christ is right there within your being reminding you,
" 'Whither thou goest, I will go. . . thy people shall be my people, ... Where thou diest will I die, and there will I be
buried.'[11] Wherever you are, *I*, the Christ, am with you. Do not
try to get *Me* to leave you because *I* will not."
    The story of Ruth and Naomi is the account of a human
being who had risen from nothing to material prosperity, family happiness, and completeness, and had lost it all except for one
thing, something as much to be disdained as a daughter-in-law,
something to be ignored as daughters-in-law are sometimes
ignored. But what was left? The Christ, the Christ that loves as
daughters-in-law sometimes do even when their love is not recognized or accepted.
    By the time the four weeks of Bible study were up, there
were thirty two people coming to the group, meeting twice a
week instead of once a week. Within four weeks more, there
were fifty people meeting, and we had to meet three times a

week. Later we secured a larger place which seated fifty five, and we met six times a week, every night of the week for sixty weeks.

Every one of those nights, the Father gave me a Bible story which has been included in *Spiritual Interpretation of Scripture.* There was not a single week that I knew what that lesson would be until God gave it to me. That same method of procedure has continued with every class.

Conscious Union with God[12]

When I began to teach the class which later was incorporated in the book *Conscious Union With God,* the first words out of my mouth were, "My conscious oneness with God constitutes my oneness with all spiritual being and idea." I did not know that until that very minute. In that minute, I was given the principle that when I am consciously one with God, I am one with every person. I am one with supply; I am one with home; I am one with companionship; and I am one with health. But all this is true only in the degree that I am one with God. In *Conscious Union With God,* there are thousands of words, but every page of it is devoted to the theme that conscious union with God constitutes oneness with all spiritual good, which manifests on the human plane in terms of human good.

So it has been that, by a willingness to teach when called upon, the lessons have been given to me, the words with which to convey the lesson, and in most cases I have been taught at the same moment the students were being taught.

The Deep Silence of My Peace[13]

The little booklet *The Deep Silence of My Peace* is another example of the spontaneity of the message. As I was walking from the hotel to the Truth Center in Seattle, Washington, where I was giving some lectures, the newspapers on the street carried four huge streamer headlines and many newsboys were out crying, "Extra! Extra!" One headline told of the loss of a battle in Korea; the second was that there was to be a national telephone strike with service on every telephone in the United States scheduled to be cut off at four o'clock in the afternoon; and finally there was to be a national railroad strike with every railroad coming to a stop at midnight.

When I arrived at the Center and stood on the platform, the air was thick with the gloom and doom of the news, which some of the people must have heard on the radio before I saw those headlines. I went to the edge of the platform and said, "Evidently these events out in the world have penetrated even into our midst." At that moment the Spirit took over and out came the rest of that lesson on peace. If you read that little booklet, you can almost hear God speak to you because God was using me as Its instrument to dissolve the fear and worry. In a few moments, those in the room were lifted up and began to realize once again their true identity.

These examples exemplify the principle that you must cast your bread upon the water if you want it to come back to you, and you must acknowledge that you already have within your consciousness the allness of God. As you are called upon, be willing to give, share, or spend so that the flow is out from you. Never take the stand that you have a demonstration to make, that you have a lack that must be fulfilled, or that you have a need of anything. Never acknowledge a need even when it seems to be there. Recognize it as an appearance, but not a reality. Although to human sense a lack might seem to be true, spiritually it is not so since "the earth is the Lord's, and the fulness thereof." All that belongs to God is yours.

I have set forth these examples to show you that unless I first acknowledged that spiritual wisdom is mine because of my oneness with God, I could not open my mouth and let it flow out. The same is true of you. If you do not acknowledge that God's wisdom is your wisdom, you will never be able to open your mouth to utter truth. If you do not acknowledge that

God's supply is yours, you will never be able to open your pocketbook and let the substance of the millions and millions of dollars that are in your consciousness flow out. You do not see them because they appear only in the order of your use of them.

Live in the Nowness of Eternity

There appears to be no end to time, but it is doled out to us second by second. We are never given five seconds all at one time to use. No, God gives us one second at a time and never any more. Look at the sunshine, the heat, and the light radiating from the sun. We have enough only for each minute. It is a continuous unfolding and disclosing from the standpoint of Infinity.

Whatever of money is in your pocket or in your bank account is usually enough for the needs of this moment. Behind it is all that the Father has. Understand that it is given to you a day's worth at a time, a month's worth, or a year's worth. You do not live on yesterday's manna, nor should you be unduly concerned about tomorrow's manna. God's grace is your sufficiency, and God's grace gives you only a second at a time in which to live. God's grace gives you only one portion of sunlight at a time; God's grace permits you to eat only one meal at a time. God's grace may be sending your supply to you in amounts of one dollar or one pound at a time or five dollars or pounds. Whatever amount it is, you should understand that it is the immediate appearing of an Infinity which underlies it.

Infinity is the measure of your capacity to be, to know, and to have. But it will appear only one grain at a time as you need it, just as our classes provide one subject at a time as needed, and as another subject is needed, it appears. If God were to give me twenty subjects in one evening, it would not bless you or me because we could not digest them any more than we could digest twenty meals in one day.

Just because you have only one second at a time to live, do

not judge by that appearance that you will not be eternally alive, because you will. The one second that you are living now is the immediacy of the infinity of time. Whatever you have of supply, home, or companionship is only the immediacy behind which Infinity is pouring Itself through in proportion to your need. As you make room for more by letting out more, more will flow.

Anyone who has ever taught will tell you that you learn only by teaching. Nobody learns by being taught. Everyone learns by teaching. The more you teach, the more you know because when you open your mouth to teach there is something that is putting more in your mouth than you ever knew. So it is that the more you spend in currency, not being wasteful but using God-given wisdom, the more the flow will be. The stronger the flow you let out, the stronger the flow that will pour in.

Cast Your Bread upon the Water

Experiencing an infinity of supply has its basis in pouring out from within. You must put your bread upon the water. You are the one who has to release it before it can return to you. You are the one who must acknowledge that you have. What do you have? You have infinity; you have eternality; you have the grace of God. What more can anyone have or want or need than the grace of God? That grace of God will appear as the measure of your health, supply, good, or companionship, and the measure of the love you have for and through one another, and flows out from the center within to the world.

Never limit the amount of love you can release out into the world. You are but the outlet for God's love, and a group of persons thus motivated could send out enough love in the world to save it. Scripture points out that "ten"[14] righteous men can save the city. A hundred persons such as you, spiritually motivated and guided, could save a nation, because it is not your love that you give out. Your love is not the measure of your capacity of giving. It is God's love that you permit to flow through you, and you can permit it to flow in an infinity of abundance, strength, and power.

Recognize the Love Flowing
to a Person as Flowing to the Christ

That infinity of love flowing forth can sometimes seem overwhelming. But if you feel you cannot handle all the love that is coming to you, you are accepting that love personally, as if that love were meant for you, and it isn't. It is really meant for God, because you of yourself could never do anything to deserve so much love. You are but an instrument for the Father and when you are thanked or when you receive love, whether from a bubbly heart or from a great big purse, it is not really meant for you as a person. It is meant for you as a representative of the power which is appearing through you.

It is very much like the attitude of a former President of the United States who was a rough diamond and a sort of good fellow. He liked to go over to the club every afternoon—this was not during the war days—and play poker with his friends. They smoked, told their stories, and took their coats off in the warm weather. One thing the President insisted on, however, was that they must address him as Mr. President because in his official capacity it was respect for his office that he demanded. For him as a man it was all right to be a hale fellow well met. But when a person was addressing him, the person had to honor his office.

That is the way spiritual teachers receive the respect and the love of their friends or students. They can take their coats off, too, and can sit around and enjoy the everyday things of life, but always remember that their real function is to reveal God. When you show that respect and love for a teacher, you are really showing it to God and to the person who is the instrument of God. Then the spiritual teacher can take any amount of adulation without having his head turned or any amount of money without using it for wrong purposes or permitting it to become the dominating motive in his life. More persons are adversely affected by wealth than by poverty. It is possible to rise above being poor but it is very difficult to rise above being rich, unless a person has been given the wisdom to know how to handle it.

God's Grace Is Always Flowing

When you give up the belief that God is withholding something from you and that you have to find some mysterious teaching or teacher or something that will make God give, you will start the flow of God in your experience. Actually God's grace is flowing now, but you yourself may be barring its entry into your experience. God is infinite good. God is the principle of life. God is the substance of life; God is the law of life; God is the reality of life; and God is the maintaining and sustaining influence of life, all without any prayers from you or me or without any treatments from you or me.

God already is about Its own business of beautifully, harmoniously, permanently, spiritually, and immortally maintaining this universe. Your acceptance of a law apart from God, even your acceptance of the belief that your sins are separating you from your good, is enough to stop the flow in your direction. It does not stop God's flow; in fact, nothing ever stops God's flow. It merely stops It from operating in your experience. That does not give you the privilege of sinning, because the Master reminds you that while there is no condemnation for your sins as long as they were performed in ignorance, now that you know, you must "go, and sin no more."[15]

Be not concerned with yesterday's sins of omission or commission. Be not concerned with yesterday's karma. Be not concerned with anything that has to do with yesterday or today, but begin this very moment with the realization that God is a living God, and God has no pleasure in your dying or being punished. As a matter of fact, the Master says, "Herein is my Father glorified, that ye bear much fruit."[16] God is not glorified in your going around in sackcloth and ashes, condemning yourself for yesterday's faults which you could not help because yesterday you could not be any better than your own state of consciousness was yesterday. God does not condemn you for that. Once you have awakened to the fact that there is a God, that God is a living being, that God is in the midst of you, and that God is an infinite power and the only power, you can then begin to rest and let the activity of God take place in you.

God Cannot Be Reached: God Is

Too many times, even those in the metaphysical world, are actually reaching out mentally as if they were trying to contact a God and thereby have God perform Its wonders of healing or of multiplying loaves and fishes for them. That is not necessary. To begin with, you can never reach God, so you might as well stop trying. The reason you can never reach God is that God is already at the center of your being, and even more than that, God already is your very life, your very soul, your very consciousness. How can you reach your own life? You *are* your own life; your life *is* you; it is all one. There is no twoness. You cannot reach up to God; you cannot reach down to God; you cannot reach within to God. God already is established as the very life of your being.

You can acknowledge this truth of God in the midst of you, and that acknowledgment will set you free from the discords of mind, body, and pocketbook.

> God already is. Since God is infinite,
> that must include my very own being because
> I cannot be outside of Infinity.
> God is. God is operating. God is functioning.
> God is about Its own business.
> God in the midst of me is mighty.

Our Work Is to Recognize Is

Once you begin to acknowledge God's presence, the mental strain is lifted, because you do not have to think thoughts to make something happen, not even right thoughts or good thoughts. The moment you realize that God is infinite, you learn that good thoughts are not any more helpful than bad thoughts are harmful. They are just not power because God alone is power.

You can think two times two are four, but that is true whether you think it or not. You can think thoughts about life being eternal, but such thoughts are not power; they do not make it so. Life was eternal in the beginning before ever time began. You can think that someone you know is spiritual, but that will not do the person any good: he was spiritual from the beginning. You can sit in a group meeting and know that all the persons there are the children of God, sharing in God's abundance and that they are the very image and likeness of God-being, and that, too, has no power; it cannot make them God's children. They already are that. They were God's children before they came into the human sense of life. In the beginning with God, the Word became flesh, and every person is that. Thinking these things does not make them true. Thinking such thoughts has the value of reminding us of that which forever has been.

The Prodigal-Experience

In the Infinite Way, the work does not really consist of changing this world, improving it, healing it, reforming it, or enriching it. The work of the Infinite Way is to come into the awareness of this world as it already is, as it always has been, and always will be in reality. If this is true, why have you and all the other people in the world not been experiencing it? Since the truth is that no man, woman, or child has ever died or sinned, why is it that we are still plagued with this belief, this appearance-world, this chaotic world?

The scriptural answer is found in the experience of the Prodigal leaving home. At one time or another we were all consciously one with God. Remember we are still one with God, but at one time we were consciously one with God, that is, we knew it. In that state of consciousness we never had to take thought for what we should eat, what we should drink, or with what we should be clothed. There never was concern or anxiety, because instead of trying to create our own world, God created it and lived it through us. In other words, there was a spiritual presence and a spiritual power functioning in and as us.

At some time and in some way, we lost that conscious unity with the Father and invented a new meaning for the word "I," The word "I" originally meant God, and the words "I Am" meant God is. Whenever the word "I" was spoken, it was really God uttering Itself. In the experience called the Prodigal-experience we decided to say, "I, Joel," "I, Bill," or "I, Mary." The result was that I, Joel, must take thought for what I should eat, drink, and with what I should be clothed because who is going to do it for me if I do not? In that state of awareness, I have completely lost sight of the truth that never at any time was I responsible for creating myself, maintaining or sustaining myself. That was always God's responsibility. Had we continued to be as little children, going to breakfast, lunch, and dinner, expecting the Father to set the table for us, this false sense of "I" would not have gotten hold of us, and we would not have started out in life by the sweat of our brow.

I, Joel, has to "die daily." I, Joel, has to give himself up. I, Joel, has to surrender himself. The Master said, "For whosoever will save his life shall lose it; but whosoever will lose his life for my sake, the same shall save it."[17] You lose your personal sense of life and the personal sense of responsibility that says you must work for it, you must pray for it, or you must treat for it, whereas all you must do is recognize and acknowledge your oneness with the source.

Living by Grace

At your present stage of development it takes a little while to realize that it is not necessary to live by the sweat of your brow. Work, yes, and the more spiritual wisdom you have the harder you will work—but not for a living. It will be for the joy of whatever it is that is given you to do. Then the living will take care of itself, and it will be abundant. When you stop working for a living—and I emphatically do not mean giving up your position or business, but entering into it with a different spirit, with the idea that this work is not being done for a living but is being done for the joy of life—supply takes care of itself more abundantly than it ever did while you thought you were working for a living.

All of this goes back to the basic premise of the Infinite Way. There is no power operating in this universe to keep you from your health or from your abundant supply. If you can accept that truth and stop working for supply, stop working for a home, stop working for companionship, and stop working for health, and instead begin to accept God's infinity, it will flow from every direction to you.

Chapter Eleven

Spiritual Vision Alone Reveals the *I Am* of Individual Being

God is the central theme of the message of the Infinite Way, but God is probably the most misunderstood word in all languages. Often in my travels, strangers ask, "What do you do? What is your business?" And I have to tell them I have no business, that I just write.

"Oh, novels? Fiction?"

Always I am in the same predicament. It is a strange thing to say, but eventually I have to tell those who ask that I write about God. Then comes the question, "What is the title of your book?" This leads me to explain that there are about twenty published books and twenty-five more coming.

"All on God?"

"Yes, I never change the subject."

That in itself is strange, but what makes it even more strange is that very few persons know what I mean when I say God. I seem to mean something different from what most of them imagine. I am sure, from my experience, that most persons not only believe in God, but to some extent they actually believe they know what God is. That, too, seems rather strange because as a rule after a year or two of study students of the Infinite Way tell me they have never known what God is and just now they are beginning to realize how difficult it is to understand the true meaning of God.

It really is difficult because regardless of what you may think about God you are bound to be wrong. You cannot be right, and you never will be right. There never will be a time when you will be correct in what you think about God. As long as you are thinking about God, you are entertaining concepts about God. Those concepts are based on your previous experience, childhood religion, or on what someone has thought, said, or written. Until a person has been a serious student of that subject for many years, God rarely becomes an actual experience. Meeting God face to face is the final word on the subject of what God is.

Opening the Soul-Center

The main function of a teacher in the activity of the Infinite Way is to open the spiritual center of the student. It is not so much the imparting of words or statements, although they play a part, but the part they play is preparatory. The teaching itself is an experience, an experience of God, awakening to God-realization those who have not had a God-experience or who may have had such an experience only occasionally but have not come to the place of more or less continuous realization.

In our classwork, a study of the writings and the recordings is important, so that the student is already somewhat familiar with Infinite Way principles before he comes to a class. It is the responsibility of the teacher to be responsive to the spiritual impulse so that the Father can give the teacher a theme or subject which is developed during the class. It may appear on the first night as one facet or one phase of the spiritual principles which are the foundation of the work, and on the second night as another phase of these soul-principles. When the recordings of the class are played afterwards it becomes clear that the entire class was centered around one subject, touched upon from different angles for the purpose of opening the spiritual center.

If Infinite Way students could learn all the words in all our books but fail to have their spiritual center opened, they would be eating husks, and living on shadows, and shadows are not very substantial food. It is necessary for our students to learn the meaning of the principles of life found in the Bible, such as "My peace I give unto you: not as the world giveth, give I unto you."[1] Our students must know the difference between *"My* peace" and the peace that the world can give. They must understand the meaning of "I have meat to eat that ye know not of."[2] They need to remember that that meat has nothing whatsoever to do with a meat market. They must understand what the Master meant when he said, "If thou knewest the gift of God, and who it is that saith to thee, Give me to drink; thou wouldest have asked of him, and he would have given thee living water. . . . But whosoever drinketh of the water that I shall give him shall never thirst."[3] Students must understand that Jesus was not talking about water in a well. Students must know the meaning of "I am the bread of life"[4] and understand that this bread has nothing to do with baker's bread.

In the Bible, we have access to a language with a hidden meaning, an esoteric, transcendental, spiritual meaning, words of which the dictionary can never give a full definition or connotation, but words which spiritual saints and seers have used.

The Nature of
Infinite Way Classwork

As we come together in a class, we share in that meat, wine, water, and bread, but it is the food the world knows not of and therefore the world cannot partake of that food. This is the mystical bread, the mystical wine, the mystical water, the mystical meat. It is the "pearl of great price,"[5] the pearl for which we should be willing to give everything that we have in order to receive. And yet it cannot be bought for money. It cannot be bought for money any more than our classwork can be bought for money. The price of truly entering into Infinite Way class-work is a desire to experience God-union, communion, and oneness. True, a person can come and sit in a class, but that does not mean he has entered the consciousness of the class. That is the reason a class is always a sacred experience. It never leaves us where it finds us because God has brought us together for the experience. How the classwork was to be conducted, who was to be in the class, and who was not was given and shown to me by God. There are no rules governing our classwork, except that we must give evidence of our desire to know God and to be willing to make some effort in the direction of finding this "pearl" that truly is without price.

The book *Living the Infinite Way*[6] has the theme of *is:* God is. Throughout the book that theme is presented from many different angles just as it was in the class from which the book was taken. But while the impartation of the letter of truth involved in that theme is taking place, something much more vital is going on.

To begin with, long before the class began, I was in prayer or communion with the members of that class. A natural question may be how could I know who the students were since I had never met them before the class. That is the way it would appear in the outer picture, but the truth is that God had already drawn us together. Long before there is any thought of a class, I am in prayer, meditation, and communion to the end that only those whom God sends will come to me, only those prepared for the message. My prayer is that those who cannot be receptive and responsive to this message be led to their teacher or teaching, so that when we finally come together as a class, it is evident that those present have been directed to the message, and I have been directed to deliver it. Under such circumstances we meet in oneness as friends. We are really closer than sisters and brothers because ours is not a brother and sister relationship merely through birth. Ours is a brother and sister relationship through our sonship in God. God is our Father.

Whether students know it or not, in coming to such a class, they have renounced human birth and accepted the truth that God is their Father. I have done the same thing, and all of us meet as children of God, spiritual brothers and sisters of one household, of one mind, in one place, and with but one purpose. That purpose is the realization, the actual demonstration, and the experience of God. That is the purpose of our class work, and that is why only those of us should be together who are drawn together in this universal sonship, daughterhood, sisterhood, or brotherhood which in truth makes us one in God.

When we come together in that kind of a relationship, we are able to demonstrate that which the entire world has sought forever and still seeks, but cannot find. We are a community of persons who cannot fight with one another, who cannot lie, cheat, steal, or defraud one another. If we even thought of attempting it, we would find ourselves struck dumb where we stand. We cannot do that because we have come together with no armor. We have come together with no weapons of offense or defense. Through prayer we have been led into the consciousness of each other as children of the one and same Father. Everyone in the class has the same Father, the same creative principle. The world seeks that but cannot find it.

Peace Comes with the
Realization of One Father

In December of 1954, I returned to Hawaii from a trip around the world. One of the first questions the students asked was, "What are the chances for world peace? What are the chances now that wars may forever be ended?" I told them to pay no attention to what they read in the newspapers because those reporting the news did not know the true situation. They were not being given the facts. The danger of war was not from any of the directions headlined in the newspapers at that time. All the danger there is at present now is in Israel,[7] Egypt, and

India. Those are the potential war spots of the world, because in those places, the age-old religious hatreds are more intense now than they have ever been, and that makes these places fertile soil for someone to come in and make trouble. It is in the Hebrew, Arab, and Hindu worlds that the entire peace effort should be centered. It is from this direction that the most serious conflicts can arise.

What makes this situation serious? The Hebrews and Arabs are age-old enemies, and nothing could be further from their beliefs than that they have a common parentage, the same Father, and that they are brothers and sisters. As long as that state of consciousness exists, there cannot be real peace. It makes no difference how many documents are signed; it makes no difference on which side the most ammunition may be. There cannot be peace between peoples who cannot come together in love, and no people can come together in love unless they belong to the same family, because there will always be differences of interest among persons. Only in a family body can there be a uniting, an actual oneness of interests, oneness of love, oneness of sharing. Everybody within a family shares with each other and they all love it, but it is that way to the fullest extent only in a family.

In order that spiritual peace be attained, it is necessary that there be but one family of men on earth and that God be recognized as the Father and the Mother of that family, the creative principle, that we all be one in Christ Jesus, that is, one in our spiritual identity. No longer shall there be Jew or Gentile, Greek or bond, slave or free, but all one in truth, one family in the Spirit.

In Infinite Way class work healings often take place: physical healings, mental, moral, sometimes financial. That is not the important thing. The important thing is that there be a transformation of consciousness in the class which may now or later result in healing. Spiritual healing is the giving up of material consciousness for spiritual consciousness. Just as material consciousness has externalized itself as a sick body or a sick pocket-book, so the attainment of spiritual consciousness externalizes itself as spiritual wholeness and spiritual supply.

Rocky, Barren, and Fertile Soil

We cannot separate a transformation of consciousness from healing because the transformation of consciousness is what appears outwardly as healing. Sometimes, for one reason or another, someone catches a glimpse of spiritual light or truth that results in a very quick healing of some nature. At other times this work is like the planting of a seed. There is the example of the three different types of soil[8] in which spiritual seed may be planted: rocky soil, barren soil, and fertile soil.

As far as the teacher is concerned, there is only one type of seed, and that is spiritual seed. From the standpoint from which the teacher is functioning, everyone in a class should receive the same benefits, because each member of the class is receiving truth and the same seed, coming out of the same prepared consciousness. The prepared consciousness of the teacher is in some measure addressing rocky soil, barren soil, and varying degrees of fertile soil. So in a class, the rocky soil probably receives nothing at all, although it is rare for rocky soil to be admitted to classwork because there are things which tend to keep such states of consciousness out before they get in. There may be some here and there, however, who have not yet caught a glimpse of the spiritual universe, but they have been working toward it, thinking about it, studying toward that end, and while they may be barren soil, they are ready for that barren soil to become fertile. That breakthrough may come in a class.

For those who are some measure of fertile soil, however, this seed takes root. Whether it shows forth outwardly as an uplift-ed consciousness and greater peace or as what appears as an instantaneous healing or whether it takes six months or a year is only an indication that the seed in consciousness must develop and bring about a change of consciousness. As soon as that change has come, then the healing is evident.

Sowing to the Flesh

"Whatsoever a man soweth, that shall he also reap. For he that soweth to his flesh shall of the flesh reap corruption, but he that soweth to the Spirit shall of the Spirit reap life everlasting."[9] If we sow to the flesh, we reap corruption; if we sow to the Spirit, we reap life everlasting. It is that simple. That is another way of describing the rocky, barren, or fertile soil. Sowing to the flesh has very little to do with immorality, sexuality, or anything that constitutes standard moral codes of conduct. Paul did not have that in mind when he spoke of sowing to the flesh.

Sowing to the flesh really means living out from a material state of consciousness that places its faith, confidence, or hope in the world of effect. Persons who believe that money is supply or that health is physical and that it has something to do with a heart, lung, stomach, and body are sowing to the flesh. Their hope is in the body, in the body being well or in the pocketbook being full. Persons who gain companionship solely from men, women, and children are sowing to the flesh. Those who derive their principal joys from the external world, whether it is the theater, movies, dances, or games are, also, sowing to the flesh.

Spiritual Sowing

Sowing to the Spirit means placing one's hope, faith, and reliance in the Invisible. In understanding and recognizing that the real issues of life are within, that supply, companionship, and health are invisible substance, and that nobody has ever seen health, supply, or companionship because these are spiritual qualities within our consciousness, we have begun to sow to the Spirit. This does not mean that we become ascetics. It does not mean that we do not enjoy the theater, music, books, or base-ball games. It means that such diversions are not the major activities of life, but are merely incidental, merely the added things found in our particular culture. Our real life consists of our inner life, the life that is lived within ourselves. When the Master went away for forty days, that is when he was really living. When he came back to heal the multitudes, that was the added thing that God had given for his earthly experience and for ours.

When we commune with the Father within in our bedroom, den, library, or garden—wherever we can find a quiet spot—that is when we are living our real life. Then when we go out into the world and act in our capacity as husbands, wives, children, neighbors, sisters, or brothers, we carry the essence of our real life out into the world to share with men and women.

Spiritual Teaching

If a teacher came to a platform as a man or woman with something to say, we might gain some knowledge from him or her, but we would not gain the real things of life: our spiritual joy, spiritual intuition, our contact with God, our health, and our supply. That, no one could get from someone who came to the platform merely to tell the audience something or to teach them something. No, a teacher on the spiritual path must live most of his or her life in aloneness, in quietness, in an inner communion with God, in prayer. Then when that teacher goes out into the world to be with students, that teacher brings the essence of God to the students' consciousness. The words that he or she speaks help but that is not it.

Not one word need be spoken. We would be able to sit in meditation, in quietness for an hour, a half hour, or an hour and a half and then go home. We would not think it strange or wonder about it at all. It would be much more natural than if the teacher were to speak on those occasions. I have had classes where we have come together and inside of fifteen or twenty minutes I have said, "Let's go home," and we all went home. There have been other classes when it seemed as if somebody were going to have to send out for the breakfast table. It just did not want to come to an end. In some cities there have been classes that began at eight o'clock in the morning and did not end until midnight. We might have a class in my room, then a class at breakfast, then a class at lunch, then off to the Center and back again, and end up with midnight coffee in a restaurant with everybody still there. That is the way the Spirit operates when we are united, not just for the sake of finding some truth but actually finding conscious communion with the truth within ourselves.

As our students go out from a class, they also have a very solemn obligation not to go out and tell others what they have learned. If they attempt to voice it, many times the right words are not on their lips. But if they have caught the essence of a class, they will be able to put something they have learned into their own words. It may be something they may not have heard in class, something that may not have been said in class, yet was imparted from the Father within to their consciousness, and they can impart that either in word, in spirit, or in healing. That is the obligation of our students.

Spiritual Discernment
Reveals Spiritual Identity

In almost every class, students are learning that God is the only power, so when individuals speak to them of their sins, their diseases, or their lacks, the students do not get into an emotional state about wanting to help them or wishing they knew enough to heal them. They learn to revert immediately to the truth they have absorbed.

Knowing that God is the only power and presence, how can

we help with something that cannot be a reality? How can we heal someone when there is no disease to be healed? How can we enrich someone when there is no lack? What we behold in the three-dimensional world through seeing, hearing, tasting, touching, and smelling is not the truth, does not bear witness to the truth, and no matter how good it is, it still has no relationship to truth.

Spiritual vision alone understands and knows that the person who reaches out for help is God's own being, God's own selfhood made manifest, God's own life expressed, God's own intelligence made evident, the very soul of God individualized as you, as me, as a patient or a student.

We acknowledge that sense testimony does not bear witness to that. We acknowledge that if I look at you through my eyes, I may see a human man or woman: good or bad, sick or well, rich or poor. If you look at me through your eyes, the most you see is a human being, even though you might go so far as to say that at least he has good intentions. But when I look out and disregard what my eyes see, there is a "still small voice"[10] within me that says, "This is my beloved Son, in whom I am well pleased."[11] Appearances do not indicate that. No, appearances do not indicate that even when people are beautiful, handsome, or physically perfect. Even then sense testimony will not show them forth as spiritual.

When the Master asked Peter, "But whom say ye that I am?"[12] it was spiritual vision that enabled him to reply, "Thou art the Christ, the Son of the living God."[12] The Master responded with, "Flesh and blood hath not revealed it unto thee, but my Father which is in heaven."[12] In other words he was telling Peter that what he saw with his eyes or heard with his ears was not what convinced him. Only the Father within could do that. It was the spiritual discernment within Peter that enabled him to know who Jesus was, and that is who I am and who you are: the Christ, the son of God, the very living witness of God's presence on earth. Spiritual discernment alone can reveal that.

Becoming Aware of the Christ-Identity

Only the inner grace of God would enable us to go into a prison and mingle with men sentenced for all kinds of crimes and yet have the divine grace to look around and say, "Thou art the Christ," not out loud, because they might think we were a little bit foolish. To ourselves, however, we can look those men and women in the eyes and realize: You are the Christ, the son of the living God, not yet aware of your true identity, but that is your true identity. Then the miracle takes place. From three years of work in prisons, I can tell of the miracles that can happen as we silently and secretly realize the Christ sitting behind the eyes of every individual.

We develop the faculty, not of looking at our patients' or students' bodies but looking at their eyes, not really looking at their eyes either, but looking behind the eyes. There we become aware of a spiritual soul gazing out at us. That is the Christ of their being which they themselves do not know exists. And what a miracle takes place! Those who have come to us do not know what we have done, but they know we have done something because they are attracted to us; they want to come to us to hear what we have to say and impart.

Healings take place in hospitals, in prisons, and in mental institutions, not by virtue of anything we may say to patients or by virtue of any truth we tell them because it is not even wise to tell truth to some people, at least not until they are well enough to have felt the effects of it so they can believe us. In teaching, however, we can impart truth to them. But otherwise what we do, we do in secret. If we do it in secret, we will watch the effects in the open.

The Responsibility of the Practitioner Is to Be a Transparency

You may have friends, relatives, patients, or students who will want to benefit by your experience in the Infinite Way.

They will say to you, "You are reading those books; you are spending hours with them; you are listening to tapes for hours; and then you go to class besides. What for? What do you get out of it? What is in it for you? Or for us and our family?" They have a right to an answer because you have no right to spend your time in much reading and much studying and much praying without being able to be the light fo the world unto those still in darkness. And so do not ever say, "No," to a request for help. Do not ever say, "Oh, why don't you see my practitioner?" or "Why don't you go to my teacher?" You accept the responsibility when you are asked for help because in the last analysis you are not being called upon to heal by your understanding, nor are you going to be called upon to heal by your spiritual power. Do not believe that you of yourself have enough understanding and do not believe that you of yourself have enough spiritual power. None of us has!

I have never yet met anyone who had enough understanding or spiritual power to heal anything. Only God has the power to remove the mist from our eyes. Only God has the power to dispel the illusions of sense, and "God is no respecter of persons."[13] God will appear through your consciousness as soon as you accept the responsibility of being a transparency. But do it in secret. Do not talk about being involved in healing work to anyone. Do not advertise it. Wait until someone comes to you and asks, and then you can say to yourself, "Thank you, Father, that the work was done before he reached here. You sent him here so that You could appear to him through my consciousness."

Let the Father Bring to You Those to Be Taught and Healed

When you go out looking for patients and students, you have a hard job to do something for them, because it is you who have to do it. But if you abide secretly in the center of your being, and someone comes to you for help, then you can say, "Thank you,

Father, You did the work before he got here, and before I could even think a right thought. Do you see how that operates? Knowing that God sent you to me, God must have put your fulfillment in my mouth; whereas if I sent for you the responsibility is up to me to be able to satisfy you. But I do not have to satisfy you; I did not send for you. I do not have to heal you; I do not have to teach you; I did not send for you. God brought us together, so that God could function in the midst of us.

When the Father sends someone to you for healing or teaching, be assured that the Father's wisdom and the Father's love will be there before the appointment to take care of the situation. God will put the words in your mouth when the patient or student comes.

Whether you are healing or teaching, you need to meditate to stay in the Spirit. Then when your patients or student are brought to you, the Father places the right words or thoughts within you, the Spirit within flows, and the work takes place. That is all an activity of God, not an activity of man. We stand foursquare with Peter and John as they stood before the Temple Gate Beautiful and said, "Ye men of Israel, why marvel ye at this? Or why look ye so earnestly on us, as though by our own power or holiness we had made this man to walk?"[14] It was the God of Abraham, and of Isaac, and of Jacob who performed this healing, and the same Spirit "that raised up Jesus from the dead. . . shall also quicken your mortal bodies."[15] There must always be a Moses, a Jesus, a John, a Paul, a you, or a me. There must always be the Christ made manifest as Jesus, or the Christ made manifest as John, Mary, or Bill. There must always be a you or a me to be the light unto those not yet awakened to their true identity.

Wear the Invisible Robe of the Spirit in Silence

We, who have received this robe of the Master, this healing consciousness, must be obedient to wear it in silence, in secrecy, and in sacredness. That is why in the Infinite Way, none of us has any title, and none of us has any robe. The reason is that we must be saints inside but just men and women outwardly. Otherwise we lose our value to the world. Those in the world may think we are something set aside or somebody set aside with special powers or special privileges. We must not appear that way to men because we are not. We are businessmen, businesswomen, or homemakers, who through devotion to God have received some measure of light. That measure of light is available to anyone who is willing to turn to that same source and be faithful until the gift comes, until the message or instruction comes showing us how we are to be fulfilled as instruments of that light within us.

Secrecy is necessary; silence is necessary. Both are embodied in sacredness. Anything we hold sacred, we hold secret. Anything we hold sacred, we hold in silence. All else we may make a public display of and show off about, but that which we consider sacred we hold very secret, very sacred, and very silent.

Our spiritual sonship is our secret. We do not tell it to the world, but we preach the gospel to those who have been led to us to receive it. We do not go out to change the world from its ways, but we do impart the truth to those who themselves want to be changed from the way they are. This, that we know in secrecy, in silence, and in sacredness, builds up into a tremendous power which is wasted if we talk about it. We waste it if we throw it around hither and yon, more especially if we spout it to those who do not wish to receive it. It is as if we hit it against a wall and it bounced back at us and gave us a good headache. No, we save the pearl of wisdom for those who can rightly value it.

When someone asks you for help do not give that person metaphysical clichés, "Oh, it isn't true," or "There is no disease in God." Do not make such statements which, while spiritually true, are not true on the human level. Otherwise you may arouse an antagonism in your patient rather than a helpful attitude. Practitioners who know this spiritual truth do not have to voice or speak it to convince a person of it. The inner silent knowing is enough.

When asked for help, it is legitimate to say, "Certainly, I will give it to you immediately, I will be with you at once"; or "I will take up work for you," or "I will go into prayer or communion for you. Call back later, or let me hear from you tomorrow." Let him know that your heart and soul and your spiritual understanding are at his service, but do not try to convert or instruct anyone while he is in pain. Further than that it is not necessary to go until there is a response, and he asks for enlightenment as to how it is done. Once you have reached that point, the outer teaching may begin. Do not attempt to teach people who are in pain, who are suffering incurable diseases, or whose mind is focused only on their outer condition until you have brought some measure of healing to them.

Until a person's own consciousness is awakened to a desire to hear the Word, let it be given to him silently, inaudibly. Let him have it in secrecy and in silence, and then when he responds, he will be able to hear and bear the words that you give him. Human beings as a rule are not able to bear the truth. They resist truth far more than they accept it. The human mind does not want to be annihilated, and spiritual truth is going to annihilate it. Through the introduction of spiritual truth into their consciousness, they are going to "die daily" until they have only that mind which was in Christ Jesus.

The human part of us knows that with enough spiritual truth our humanhood will be wiped out, and as human beings we do not like it. Some persons like baseball games too much to give them up; some like radio or television; others like novels; and still others like dancing. They just are not ready to have those things taken from them. Spiritual realization is going to take the desire for most of the things of the world away from them, even the good things in the world.

As this spiritual life touches individual consciousness, an inordinate desire for many social activities goes out the window.

If we were to say that to these persons in advance, they would respond, "Why should I give them up?" We would have no answer, because humanly there is nothing wrong about them. It is only that too much participation in these activities infringes on our spiritual life. Spiritually they can become a hindrance to our spiritual development and eventually they no longer appeal to us.

The truth about God, the Christ, the son of God, that truth is the great pearl. It has been known as the great pearl throughout all ages. Who would show a priceless pearl to someone who is not a connoisseur of gems. It would just be a waste, wouldn't it? And so it is with this. We do not take out our pearls to show to the man in the street. When we find someone in distress, we may voice something or we may give that person a pamphlet or a book, but then we stop there, until there is some response.

This work may return to you not only as great spiritual prosperity, but it may also result in economic prosperity. That is not why you come to it. You come to it seeking the light. Therefore, you need not seek an audience; you need not seek a public; you need not seek a practice or a student body: you need only fulfill yourself with the spirit of God, the word of God, and then the Father that sees in secret sends those who are ready for the message.

TAPE RECORDED EXCERPTS
Prepared by the Editor

Let us never forget that "eternal vigilance is the price of liberty." While conforming to our responsibilities as citizens, let our real work be that spiritual vigilance that accepts only one power and recognizes the nonpower of that which would enslave mankind.

The Importance of Accepting the Responsibilities of Citizenship

"Nowhere have any people been able to maintain their free-

dom for any great length of time. . . . A few centuries seems to
be about the limit that people can hold on to a free system of
government. . . . Eventually nations lose their freedom either to
a political dictatorship or a religious dictatorship. One or the
other always swallows up men's freedom.

"Unless there is some spiritual experience in the near future,
that same condition is going to continue. Country after country will lose its freedom including this one. . . .There are reasons
why freedom cannot be maintained in any country. First, and
probably the most important, is mental inertia. People just do
not care about freedom while they have it, as long as their
human needs are being met. Let them earn enough to get by
and keep them reasonably occupied with baseball, football,
wrestling, television, radio, or some other external amusement,
and you have them body and soul. . . .

"People pay no attention to the fact that their liberties are
menaced, that their freedom and economic well-being are menaced because nobody is interfering with their pleasure at the
moment and nobody is interfering with their profit at the
moment. . . . The entire world is being threatened. . . but threatened most of all by ourselves and our unwillingness to think."

Joel S. Goldsmith, "The Mysticism and Metaphysics of the
Infinite Way," *The 1959 Hawaiian Village Closed Class*,
Tape 1:2..

Chapter Twelve

God Alone Is Power

Out of depths of the silence, out of the infinite withinness, come the joy, the peace, and the harmony of our daily life. Most persons in the world miss much of this harmony because they are seeking their good outside themselves. They believe that their good can come to them from somebody, from something, or from somewhere other than their consciousness. For thousands of years people have been seeking health, wealth, peace, safety, security out here in the world, thinking that these could come through men, organizations, or places. It is not true and never has been true. The kingdom of God which is the kingdom of Allness has to be found within individual being.

If heretofore you have been expecting good to come to you, be willing this very minute to give up all thought of any good coming to you at any time from any place, person, situation, or condition in this world. The longer you expect good to come to you, the longer you will be waiting for it and the closer will come the realization that it is not going to come. It never has for anyone. It never will come *to* you. But if you can give up all thoughts, hopes, and desires of getting, receiving, or achieving good, and understand that you, yourself, are the place where God fulfills Himself, you will be that place where God flows through to all those who do not yet know their true identity.

The Master Revealed Our True Identity

At one time I was asked to speak with two ministers on the subject of meditation and, if possible, to help them with their practice of meditation. One of them asked, "Do you believe that in this short time we have together today you can teach us how to meditate?" I told them I could not answer that question until they answered a couple of other questions. Then I would be able to tell them very quickly whether or not they could achieve meditation and the fruits of meditation in such a short period. First of all, I asked, "Do you believe that Jesus Christ is the son of God?

Very quickly came the response, "Why, certainly. Yes, indeed, of course. How can you question that?"

"I was not questioning it. I was just laying the foundation for another question. Do you believe that I am the son of God?" Then one minister looked at me rather shocked. Even though he was afraid to answer in the negative, I persisted, "It is very necessary that we have an answer. Do you believe that I am the son of God?" Since he could not say, "Yes," I had to ask, "Do you believe in the teaching of Jesus Christ?" His enthusiastic, "Yes," was just as great as his enthusiasm when he acknowledged that Jesus was the son of God. "No," I said, "you do not entirely accept the teaching of Jesus Christ. A part of it you omit."

"No, no, I accept it all."

"How about this statement, 'Call no man your father upon the earth: for one is your Father, which is in heaven?[1] Do you accept that?"

He caught that instantly. "Why, certainly, that is exactly what Jesus was teaching two thousand years ago."

So I continued with another question: "'The Spirit itself beareth witness with our spirit, that we are the children of God: And if children, then heirs; heirs of God, and joint-heirs with

Christ.'[2] If you are children of God, if you are heirs of God, if you are joint-heirs with Christ in God, now what would you like to have added to you? What do you hope can come to you now? What can be given to you now? You already have all. 'Son, thou art ever with me, and all that I have is thine.'[3] If you are children of God, if you are heirs, then by divine inheritance you have all that the Father has. What does the Father have? 'The earth is the Lord's, and the fulness thereof,'[4] and all that is yours as joint-heirs with Christ.

"When you can accept this teaching of the Master revealing your true identity as children of God, offspring of the one great King, the Father of all, the creative principle of all, and recognize yourselves to be heirs of God, how can you then think any longer in terms of earning a living by the sweat of your brow or in terms of getting something from someone, many someones, or even from the government? Do you not see that salvation is individual, that no one can bring it to you? You, yourself, must accept it by an act of consciousness, by an act of 'dying' daily and being reborn of the Spirit.

"If you are willing to 'die' to your humanhood in this moment, if you are willing to 'die' to that mortality which is forever seeking something or someone, you permit yourself to be reborn of the Spirit. If in your consciousness you can acknowledge, 'Yes, I can accept my divine sonship. I can accept the divine heritage of a child of God. I can accept God as my only Father, my only creative principle, my maintaining and sustaining life,' if you can do that, meditation should be easy because then you can forever drop the desire for something or someone and permit yourself to be an instrument through which all the heavenly riches pour from you and through you out into the world of men."

Being an Instrument Through Which the Light Shines

This world is full of persons who have not yet become aware of their true identity. The world is full of those who do not yet know that they are joint-heirs with Christ to all the heavenly riches. They are in spiritual darkness, and because they are in spiritual darkness, they expect good to come to them. They think that "man, whose breath is in his nostrils"[5] can give them peace, safety, security, prosperity, joy, health, harmony, wholeness, and completeness. But you, the disciples of the Christ, you who have turned to the great master and have learned that Christhood is your true identity, that the son of God is your very being, you know that that makes you the light of the world.

You can no more expect good to come to you than the Master Christ Jesus did. At no time was he praying for anything for himself, asking for anything for himself, expecting anything to come to him for himself. Why should he? He knew that he was the son of God, the son of the most High. All that the Father had was his. The Father within him even multiplied loaves and fishes for the multitudes, healed the sick, opened the eyes of the blind, and raised the dead. By those very deeds the Master proved that he was the son through which all these blessings were given to the world.

But the Master admonished his followers, "Call no man your father upon the earth: for one is your Father, which is in heaven." As you accept God as your Father so also do you accept yourself as the son, and then you assume the position that Jesus assigned to you: "Greater works than these shall he do."[6] Why? Because your Father and my Father are the same Father. That Father is within you and that Father does the same works in you as the Father does in me, or as he did in Peter, John, Matthew, or Mark.

Do you remember the scene at the Temple Gate Beautiful in Jerusalem where the lame man was sitting at the gate? Peter and John walked by and spoke to the cripple, "Silver and gold have I none; but such as I have give I thee. . . . Rise up and walk."[7] And the lame man did; he leaped up.

Evidently those who witnessed this were astounded. Peter said, "Ye men of Israel, why marvel ye at this? Or why look ye so earnestly on us, as though by our own power or holiness we had made this man to walk?"[8] The same Spirit that "raised up Christ from the dead shall also quicken your mortal bodies by his Spirit that dwelleth in you."[9] The same Father that in Jesus was called "the Father within," healed the sick. That same Father, the God of Isaac, the God of Abraham, the God of Jacob, through Peter and John, healed; that same Father later healed through Paul, showing truly that the Father is "no respecter of persons."[10]

Heirs of God

Wherever an individual can open his consciousness to the truth that God is the Father, the Power, the Presence, the Light, and that every person individually is the son of the most High, heir to all those heavenly riches, heir to all of God's spiritual capacity, the same feeding of the multitudes or healing of the sick will take place through him or through you and through me. It must be recognized that there have been spiritually illumined people in all ages before and since the Master. But what constituted the illumination of their being? Was it not the realization of their true identity? Nothing else could have done it.

Once we know our true identity as sons of God, bit by bit we lose the traces of mortality which are evidenced as sin, disease, death, poverty, lack, and limitation. These drop off step by step in proportion as we understand God to be the reality and cause of our being, that which created us from the womb. Mankind likes to believe that man was created in sin and brought forth in iniquity, but scripture indicates that we are spiritually conceived and spiritually brought forth as children of God.

It is not a simple thing to turn from being a beggar to being an heir. It is not an easy matter to turn from begging and pleading with God and pleading with men and women for a favor here and a favor there to turning around and realizing we are not beggars: we are heirs to everything that the Father has, to every capacity, every ability, to the fullness of the Godhead bodily. It is not easy to make that transition, but it can be done because it has been done.

It can be done, but it requires steadfastness because one hour after you finish reading this letter, a temptation will come to you reminding you that you lack something, want something, need something, desire something, and in that same hour it will be necessary to turn upon that.

"Get thee behind me, Satan."[11]
I have no needs, no desires, no requests,
because all that the Father has is already mine.
Spiritual sonship is my true relationship
to the Father, and I can be patient and wait
day by day until under God's grace the fullness of
His capacity begins to flow through me.
Why should I marvel, then, as if I of my own
understanding or my own power had done this thing?
I am nothing, but the Father within me,
and my recognition of the Father within me,
is all things and does the work.

The Miracle-Principle

Through this understanding we come to one of the major principles in the Infinite Way: one power. That one principle of itself will make miracle changes in your experience. Give up consciously the belief that there is a great power called God that you can use for the overcoming of negative powers called sin, disease, lack, or limitation.

Accept the truth that God is infinite; therefore, God-power is infinite, and there is no other power. Accept that in your consciousness and realize that anything that is appearing in your experience as an enemy, whether it is a person, a condition, a disease, or a desire, has no power to do anything, be anything, to continue to do anything, or to continue to be anything. If these suggestions have been accepted heretofore as powers in your experience, understand now that there is but one power and that power is God, infinite good.

Besides that power of good, there is no other power, just as besides God, there is no other God. Withdraw power from anything appearing in your experience to which you have given power. Withdraw power from the sins or the diseases of your body or the erroneous thoughts of your mind; withdraw power from this world. Realize that power is not in you or in me, as if by your understanding or mine, we could do something; but realize that all power is in God, God operating in your consciousness and mine, within you and within me.

Practicing the
Principle of One Power

Take any specific form of error that disturbs you, whether it appears as a person, a false appetite, or as a disease, and begin at once to realize, "Thou couldest have no power at all against me, except it were given thee from above."[12] God alone is power. Power has been given to people, to nations, to armies, and to bombs, but long ago Hezekiah knew what was wrong and said of the enemy, "With him is an arm of flesh,"[13] meaning that the enemy had only physical power, "but with us is the Lord our God to help us."[13] They had the one and only power. Physical might is not power; mental might is not power. "Not by might, nor by power, but by my spirit, saith the Lord of hosts."[14]

Begin to recognize that neither things nor thoughts have power: only God is power, only the divine consciousness of this universe is power, only the Infinite Invisible is power. Nothing that can be seen, heard, tasted, touched, smelled, or thought is power.

"And which of you with taking thought can add to his

stature one cubit?"[15] "Thou canst not make one hair white or black."[16] "If ye then be not able to do that thing which is least, why take ye thought for the rest?"[17] Things and thoughts are power only in the third dimensional realm that accepts them as power. But once you have perceived that God is invisible spirit, the causative principle of the universe, and that all cause, all power, all activity, and all substance are in God, never again can you fear what man can do to you, what mortal mind can do, or what any mortal condition can do to you because you will recognize that all mortality is without power. The fault has been in accepting the world belief that there is a power outside yourself. The Master explained it when he said, "Not that which goeth into the mouth defileth a man; but that which cometh out of the mouth, this defileth a man."[18] It is what comes out of your consciousness that defileth, and nothing in the external realm can do it. It is only what exists in the internal realm that is power.

When you accept God, the Father within you, as the only power, you come into the spiritual healing ministry, which is a state of consciousness in which you do not use God or Truth to heal disease, in which you do not use any power to heal disease, but in which you rise into the awareness of God as infinite good, a state of consciousness in which nothing but God is power or has power, nothing but God is or has law. When you understand God as the one power and the one law you have no other powers or laws. There are no lesser laws or lesser powers to be overcome. You stand firm in your realization: God alone is power.

Symbols of a Lack of Understanding

What of these sins, diseases, and deaths in the world? Do they not exist? Certainly, they exist. They exist in the same sense that the devil exists. The devil is but a symbol or a belief of a presence or power apart from God. The devil is a symbol or a belief of opposition to God. That is all the devil is: a symbol, a belief. That is all sin, disease, and lack are—symbols of the belief in a power apart from God. When you have no power apart from God, you have no symbols: you have reality. The symbols of a lack of understanding disappear in your enlightenment.

There is no sin as such. There is no disease as such. These exist as symbols of a faith or belief in a presence and power apart from God. They exist as evidence of a lack of understanding. When there is no lack of understanding, there are no symbols. When there is an understanding of God through which this all-ness flows, you lose those symbols or beliefs called sin, disease, fear, lack, or limitation.

There Is No Fear
When Anchored in God

Of all these symbols, fear, perhaps more than any other, represents a deep conviction that there is no God. It is the symbol of a lost faith and a lost hope in God. No one who believes in God has ever feared. No one. When you have experienced fear it has been because of your unbelief in God. True, you may have paid lip service and said, "Oh, yes, I believe in God," but you could not have believed in Him very much, because where there is a conviction that there is God, there is no fear. Just as the man with much money does not fear poverty, so a person with much realization of God does not fear anything or anybody in the realm of effect.

Fear is a symbol of lost hope and lost faith in God. With the restoration of faith and a conviction that God is, fear disappears. No one has ever feared who has known God. No one who has known God has ever feared to live, nor has he ever feared to pass on. Even death is not an enemy when one knows God, for like David it is recognized, "Yea, though I walk through the valley of the shadow of death, I will fear no evil: for thou art with me."[19] Even in the valley of the shadow of death, there is no fear. Why should anyone fear life or death if God is there? Why should one fear being in any place if God is there? Why should one fear even disease if God is there? The fears entertained about life, health, and supply are in direct proportion to a lack of faith and understanding of God as infinite and omnipresent.

It becomes your function as children of God to awaken. "Awake thou that sleepest, and arise from the dead, and Christ shall give thee light."[20] Awake right now to the truth that God is. Become convinced that God is, and then all else disappears from your experience except the continuous beauty and harmony of spiritual existence. It is not necessary to fight disease. It is not necessary to fight sin. It is necessary only to accept God, a living God in the midst of you. The acceptance and realization of God is the instantaneous dispelling of fear, of sin, of disease, and more especially of lack and limitation.

It is important to withdraw fear from the realm of effect and place power in the invisible. Understand that there is no power out here in person, place, or thing. Recognize that power does not exist in effect: it exists in the invisible, and that invisible power is the influence unto the effect, always good, harmonious, and perfect.

Instruments of Grace

The oft-repeated example of your hand is a good one. Is your hand a good hand or a bad hand? You can have but one answer. It is neither. There is no quality of good in your hand and there is no quality of bad in it. It is just a hand, that is all. But how about when it pets or when it punches? How about when it gives or when it steals? Is the hand doing that? No, the hand is but an instrument for consciousness. There is no good and no evil out here. Everything is as dead as your hand, but everything responds to the inner impulse which is God. It may also respond to another impulse, the impulse of belief.

If you accept the belief in two powers, then your hand may

in one instance pet and in another instance punch. When you are allowing it to be under the influence of two powers, those powers can be both good and evil, and so the hand may respond to either impulse. When you have withdrawn your faith in two powers and acknowledge God as the only power, however, then the hand becomes the living instrument of God, and it loses it power to punch or to steal. It has left only the power now to give, to share, to pet. That is not true, however, as long as you entertain the belief in two powers. Then, the hand can do good and it can do evil. The mind can think good and it can think evil as long as you accept two powers.

The moment you have accepted God as the one and only infinite Being, you have accepted grace, and grace operates only as good. Under grace, your mind, body, hand, and feet become the instruments of divine grace. Furthermore, there is no other power to use them because you have not accepted any other power. You have rejected all power but God. You have given your mind, soul, and body as instruments to be fulfilled by God.

Rejecting the Belief in Two Powers

Disease in the body is the belief of being under material law, the law of two powers. Under the belief in two powers, you may be used by the power of health today and the power of disease tomorrow. When, however, you reject all power except the power of God, you then let God become that which fills your body and you realize:

My body is the temple of the living God.
Because my body is the temple of the living God,
only God has access to this body.
Only God can fill it with Its own Spirit,
with Its own life,
for there is no other.

Until you consciously reject the belief in two powers, you will have a power out here to act upon the body, able to make it sick or well or to make it age. When you reject that suggestion, your body loses its power to become sick, and it loses it power to age. It becomes an instrument for life eternal. It becomes an instrument for the showing forth of God's glory. "The heavens declare the glory of God; and the firmament sheweth his handiwork."[21] The heavens are nothing of themselves and the earth is nothing of itself, but the heavens declare the glory of God and the earth showeth forth His handiwork. This is true of your life, your being, and your body. Your life, your mind, your soul, your being, and your body are here for one purpose: to show forth, not your health, but His glory. Think of that.

God's Glory Made Manifest

You are not to fight disease in the body: you are to recognize and submit your body to God. The heavens declare the glory of God: they do not declare their own glory; the heavens do not say, "We are beautiful"; the stars do not say, "Look how we shine." It is God's glory that is being shown forth through the heavens; it is God's glory that is being shown forth through the firmament; it is God's glory that is being made manifest in your body as health, wisdom, guidance, and direction.

God is showing Itself forth in you, through you, as you, as your very being—God, the Father, and God, the son, are one and the same. So God, the Father, is appearing on earth as God, the son. God, the Father, and God, the son, are the same. Eternal life in heaven is eternal life on earth. Eternal being in heaven is eternal being on earth. I and the Father are one. God is the Father and God is the son, the one life, the one being, the one source, the one soul, the one body, the Father and the son.

As you recognize that, you give up the thought of good coming to you, health coming to you, or wealth coming to you, and realize that you are the instrument through which these flow. You are God's instrument. It is you who show forth His handiwork, when you have withdrawn from your consciousness this world belief in two powers: a God and a devil, an immortal and a mortal, a good and an evil. These exist on earth in human consciousness because of the basic belief in two powers.

Give up the belief in two powers, and you have only one power, and it is in the invisible. Then everything in the visible shows forth God's handiwork, reflects it, or expresses it. Everything—your mind, your soul, your body—can show forth God's glory once you realize the infinite and omnipresent nature of God within your own being. With that awareness, something new begins to take place in the mind. No longer do you take thought for making things happen, but now thought comes to you from the Infinite Within revealing the harmony in this universe.

God Utters His Word

"The word of God is quick, and powerful, and sharper than any two-edged sword."[22] Very often we think we can speak the word of God. We can't. Only God can utter His word. Only God can utter His voice. God speaks: we hear. When we hear the word of God, when we hear within us the "still small voice,"[23] that Word is power, that Word is quick and sharp and powerful, and It does go right to the center of being. Let us be sure, however, that we are not thinking of that Word as words we read in a book, but the word of God which comes to us from within our own being.

The truth that you speak or the truth that you read is not power any more than anything else in the realm of effect is power. The power is in God uttering Itself through you as speech.

If I am in a receptive state of consciousness, and the word of God comes through me, it is quick and sharp and powerful, and you can be assured, if it is the word of God coming

through, it heals the sick, multiplies loaves and fishes, and raises the dead. If I merely pick up a book to read or voice something, that is not the word of God; that is not what was promised to be quick and sharp and powerful.

Importance of Listening

When you are developing your spiritual life, it is important
to spend a short time in reading the words of wisdom that have
come from the spiritually illumined of all ages. Spend some
time reading and pondering those things, but then give the
biggest amount of time to listening within your own self for that
is where the kingdom of God is. Listen within yourself until the
day comes when you are able to be receptive and responsive to
that inner presence. Then when It speaks to you, as It did with
Peter and John, It does the miracle-works of regeneration. It
restores "the years that the locust hath eaten."[24] It does, not you,
not I: It, the divine presence and power within you, this Infinite
Invisible, this Thing that wells up within you and then flows out
from you, It does the works.

Instead of persisting in a battle between good health and
bad health, between goodness and badness, between abundance
and lack, give up this struggle. Acknowledge here and now that
you are not under the law of cause and effect. At this instant of
accepting your divine sonship, you are under grace. You do not
believe that the son of God is under the law of cause and effect.
You do not believe that the son of God can be influenced by
human motives, human beliefs, or human powers.

Not Struggle, but Recognition,
Acceptance, and Realization

In this instant of your rebirth you know that you are accepting for yourself the reign of grace in your experience. Life harmonious is the gift of God, not to be earned or won, not to be

battled for, but to be accepted.

"Wherefore come out from among them, and be ye separate."[25] No longer battle for your rights, but live under divine grace. No longer take up the sword of this world: the sword of defense or the sword of offense, nor even the armor of defense, but take up the sword of the Spirit which is the realization of divine grace. Accept the teaching of the Master that "it is your Father's good pleasure to give you the kingdom."[26] What you have to do is to accept it, not fight, not battle, not struggle, not strive to achieve it: accept it.

Our terminology is all wrong when we think of a search for God or a struggle for God. The truth is the other way around. It is God that is struggling to reach us, and we are running away so fast He cannot catch up with us. We do not give Him time to catch up, although He is ever present. But we are so busy struggling, so busy fighting, so busy thinking that we do not get quiet enough to hear God utter Himself within us and reveal to us His presence and power, saying to us: "Son, I have always been with you. I was with you before Abraham was. I will be with you until the end of the world. I will never leave you or forsake you." And all the while God is there speaking, we are engaging in a search for God, for the God that is hidden within our own being. We search and struggle for God when God is saying, "From the beginning I was with you. I am ever with you. I will always be with you."

Recognition, acceptance, and realization are three important words. We have to begin recognizing God; we have to begin accepting God in the midst of us; we have to begin realizing divine grace. "Herein is my Father glorified that ye bear much fruit."[27] Do you see that? You do not have to be like Francis Thompson in "The Hound of Heaven" and have to have God hound you all over the world before you let Him catch up with you. You do not have to get down into the gutter where he did, where he could not run any further and God finally caught him. You do not have to run away from God. You can stand still. You can accept the divine government right where you are. You can accept your divine sonship.

You can accept God as the only influence in your life and you can learn to look out at all men and women and say, "I love you, and I will share with you and bear with you, but I don't fear you. There isn't anything you have that I want because all that the Father has is mine. I live under grace, not under fear, not under the law, not under cause and effect, not under karma. I live under grace. Though my 'sins be as scarlet, they shall be as white as snow.'²⁸" The man of scarlet is dead. That was the man who lived under the law of Moses, the law of cause and effect.

But the son of God is born who lives by grace, not by might, not by power, but by My Spirit, and that son of God lives forever with those of the hearing ear. That son of God lives forever in such a way that the spiritual impulse within is understood and heard as it comes into the without. "I live; yet not I, but Christ liveth in me."²⁹ If that is true, it can be true only if you can learn to listen, to feel, to let It flow instead of trying to express personal power or personal dominion.

If you live in a constant attitude of listening, as if you were expecting your guidance and direction, protection, and all good from within instead of from without, that is exactly how your life becomes, like Paul's! "I live, yet not I; but Christ liveth in me." You are the instrument but only by listening and listening. Then divine grace takes over, and that grace does not fight evil, sin, or disease. It just lives Its own life and never finds opposition, just as God finds no opposition. There is no opposite to the Infinite. There is no opposition to Infinity. There is nothing existing outside of Infinity if Infinity is infinite. Within that Infinity, all is of the nature of the Divine.

This truth, backed by scripture, becomes true only in your experience in the degree, first of all, of your acceptance of it, and secondly, in proportion as you spiritually discern it. This spiritual discernment comes to you through meditation. You can accept this truth intellectually, but you cannot demonstrate it until it has gone deeper than the intellect and has actually become a part of your inner discernment and realization. Meditation is the way of that.

About the Series

The 1971 through 1981 *Letters* will be published as a series of eleven fine-quality soft cover books. Each book published in the first edition will be offered by Acropolis Books and The Valor Foundation, and can be ordered from either source:

ACROPOLIS BOOKS, INC.
8601 Dunwoody Place
Suite 303
Atlanta, GA 30350-2509
(800) 773-9923
acropolisbooks@mindspring.com

THE VALOR FOUNDATION
1101 Hillcrest Drive
Hollywood, FL 33021
(954) 989-3000
info@valorfoundation.com

Scriptural References and Notes

CHAPTER ONE

1. Matthew 16:13,14.
2. Matthew 16:15.
3. Matthew 16:16,17.
4. John 9:25.
5. Deuteronomy 6:5.
6. Exodus 3:5.
7. Psalm 139:8-10.
8. Psalm 91:1,10.
9. John 15:5,6.
10. Acts 10:34.
11. John 10:30.
12. Luke 15:31.
13. Matthew 19:17.
14. Romans 7:19.
15. Luke 17:21.
16. Ephesians 5:14.
17. John 17:3.
18. Galatians 2:20

CHAPTER TWO

1. Hebrews 13:5.
2. Matthew 28:20.
3. Exodus 14:13.
4. John 10:10.
5. Isaiah 45:2.
6. Psalm 118:6.
7. II Chronicles 32:8.

CHAPTER THREE

1. I Timothy 6:10.
2. Philippians 2:5.
3. Matthew 4:4.
4. Matthew 5:20.
5. I John 4:11.
6. John 20:13.
7. Matthew 6:32.
8. Luke 12:32.
9. I Corinthians 3:16.
10. Isaiah 55:1.
11. Ezekiel 18:32.
12. John 8:58.
13. Hebrews 13:5.
14. Matthew 28:20.
15. John 10:10.
16. Psalm 139:7.
17. Matthew 6:27.
18. Matthew 5:36.
19. John 8:32.
20. John 10:30.

CHAPTER FOUR

1. John 5:30.
2. John 14:10.
3. John 14:16,17.
4. Matthew 6:33.
5. John 14:27.

6. Exodus 13:21.
7. I Kings 17:13.
8. I Kings 17:6.
9. Matthew 4:4.
10. Matthew 6:19.
11. Proverbs 3:5,6.
12. Matthew 10:19,20.
13. Acts 1:24.
14. Isaiah 26:3.
15. Isaiah 30:15.
16. John 4:32.
17. Exodus 3:14.
18. John 10:10.
19. John 6:35.
20. John 11:25.
21. John 14:6.
22. Isaiah 45:2.
23. Matthew 28:20.
24. John 8:58.
25. Hebrews 13:5.
26. I John 4:4.
27. Job 23:14.
28. Psalm 138:8.
29. Hebrews 11:3.
30. John 19:11.
31. Psalm 127:1.

CHAPTER FIVE

1. John 10:30.
2. John 8:58.
3. Galatians 2:20.
4. John 5:30.
5. Isaiah 2:22.
6. Acts 3:12.

7. Acts 3:13.
8. Matthew 6:9.
9. Romans 8:11.
10. I Kings 19:12.
11. Luke 12:30,32.
12. Luke 17:21.
13. John 14:16,17.
14. Luke 10:17.
15. Luke 10:20.
16. II Corinthians 5:1.
17. John 4:32.

CHAPTER SIX

1. Matthew 6:33.
2. Job 19:26.
3. John 14:27.
4. Genesis 14:20.
5. Romans 8:17.
6. Matthew 23:37.
7. Psalm 24:1.
8. Luke 15:31.
9. Psalm 82:6.
10. Romans 8:16,17.
11. John 14:6.
12. Matthew 11:28.

CHAPTER SEVEN

1. Isaiah 2:22.
2. John 5:30.
3. John 5:31.
4. John 14:10.
5. John 10:30.
6. I John 4:4.
7. Exodus 20:4,5.
8. Joshua 24:15.
9. Matthew 6:30.
10. Matthew 17:20.
11. Matthew 9:28.
12. Matthew 13:58.
13. Psalm 23:4.
14. Isaiah 43:2.
15. Romans 8:11.
16. Luke 4:8.
17. Luke 15:31.
18. Matthew 26:52.

CHAPTER EIGHT

1. Romans 8:8,9,14.
2. John 4:10,14.
3. Isaiah 2:22.
4. Matthew 7:14.
5. Luke 9:59-61.
6. Luke 9:62.
7. Psalm 23:4.
8. Hebrews 13:5.
9. Luke 22:42.
10. I Kings 19:12.
11. Psalm 46:10.
12. Psalm 24:1.

CHAPTER NINE

1. John 18:36.
2. Luke 17:21.
3. Alfred, Lord Tennyson.
4. Job 22:21.
5. Proverbs 3:6.
6. John 17:3.
7. Psalm 37:25.
8. I John 4:8.
9. Psalm 24:1.
10. Luke 15:31.
11. Exodus 16:19,20.
12. By the author.
13. Galatians 2:20.
14. Philippians 4:13.
15. Isaiah 45:2.

CHAPTER TEN

1. Matthew 14:17.
2. John 14:27.
3. Luke 4:8.
4. Matthew 6:25.
5. Matthew 6:32.
6. By the author.
7. Isaiah 2:22.
8. John 18:36.
9. John 1:17.
10. Ruth 1:16.
11. Ruth 1:17.
12. By the author.
13. By the author.
14. Genesis 18:32.
15. John 8:11.

16. John 15:8.
17. Luke 9:24.

CHAPTER ELEVEN

1. John 14:27.
2. John 4:32.
3. John 4:10,14.
4. John 6:35.
5. Matthew 13:46.
6. By the author.
7. Ed. Note: This class was given in 1955.
8. Mark 4:5-16.
9. Galatians 6:7,8.
10. I Kings 19:12.
11. Matthew 3:17.
12. Matthew 16:15,16,17.
13. Acts 10:34.
14. Acts 3:12.
15. Romans 8:11.

CHAPTER TWELVE

1. Matthew 23:9.
2. Romans 8:16,17.
3. Luke 15:31.
4. Psalm 24:1.
5. Isaiah 2:22.
6. John 14:12.
7. Acts 3:6.
8. Acts 3:12.
9. Romans 8:11.
10. Acts 10:34.
11. Luke 4:8.

12. John 19:11.
13. II Chronicles 32:8.
14. Zechariah 4:6.
15. Luke 12:25.
16. Matthew 5:36.
17. Luke 12:26.
18. Matthew 15:11.
19. Psalm 23:4.
20. Ephesians 5:14.
21. Psalm 19:1.
22. Hebrews 4:12.
23. I Kings 19:12.
24. Joel 2:25.
25. II Corinthians 6:17.
26. Luke 12:32.
27. John 15:8.
28. Isaiah 1:18.
29. Galatians 2:20.

Joel S. Goldsmith
Tape Recorded Classes
Corresponding to the
Chapters of this Volume

Tape recordings may be ordered from

THE INFINITE WAY
PO Box 2089, Peoria AZ 85380-2089
Telephone 800-922-3195 Fax 623-412-8766

E-mail: infiniteway@earthlink.net
www.joelgoldsmith.com
Free Catalog Upon Request

Chapter 6:   The Substance of All Good
               1951 Second Portland Series, Tape 1:2.

Chapter 7:   Freedom Through Grace
               1951 Second Portland Series, Tape 2:2.

Chapter 8:   The Spiritual Life
               1951 Second Portland Series, Tape 3:1 & 2.

Chapter 9:   Seek The Substance, Not The Form
               1955 Capetown Series, Tape 1:2.

Chapter 10:   Start The Flow To God
               1955 Capetown Series, Tape 2:1.

Chapter 11:   Spiritual Vision Alone Reveals
               The *I Am* of Individual Being
               1955 Capetown Series, Tape 2: 1 & 2.

Chapter 12:   God Alone Is Power
               1955 Capetown Series, Tape 1:1.